Real World Colouring Book

For Advanced Users & Adults

50 Images

Created From Real Life Photos For You To Colour As You Please.

ISBN 978-0-359-93589-5
90000
9 780359 935895

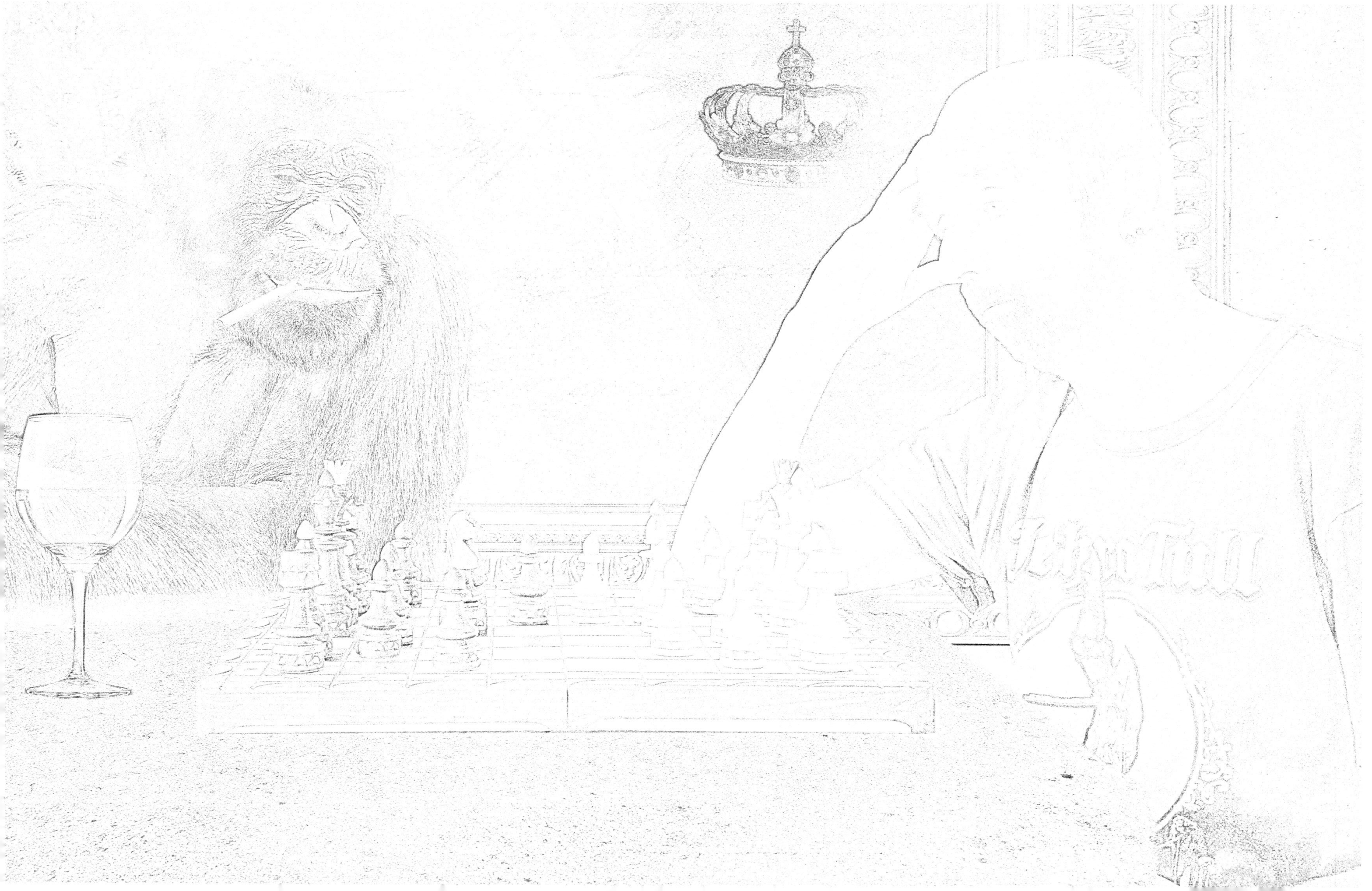

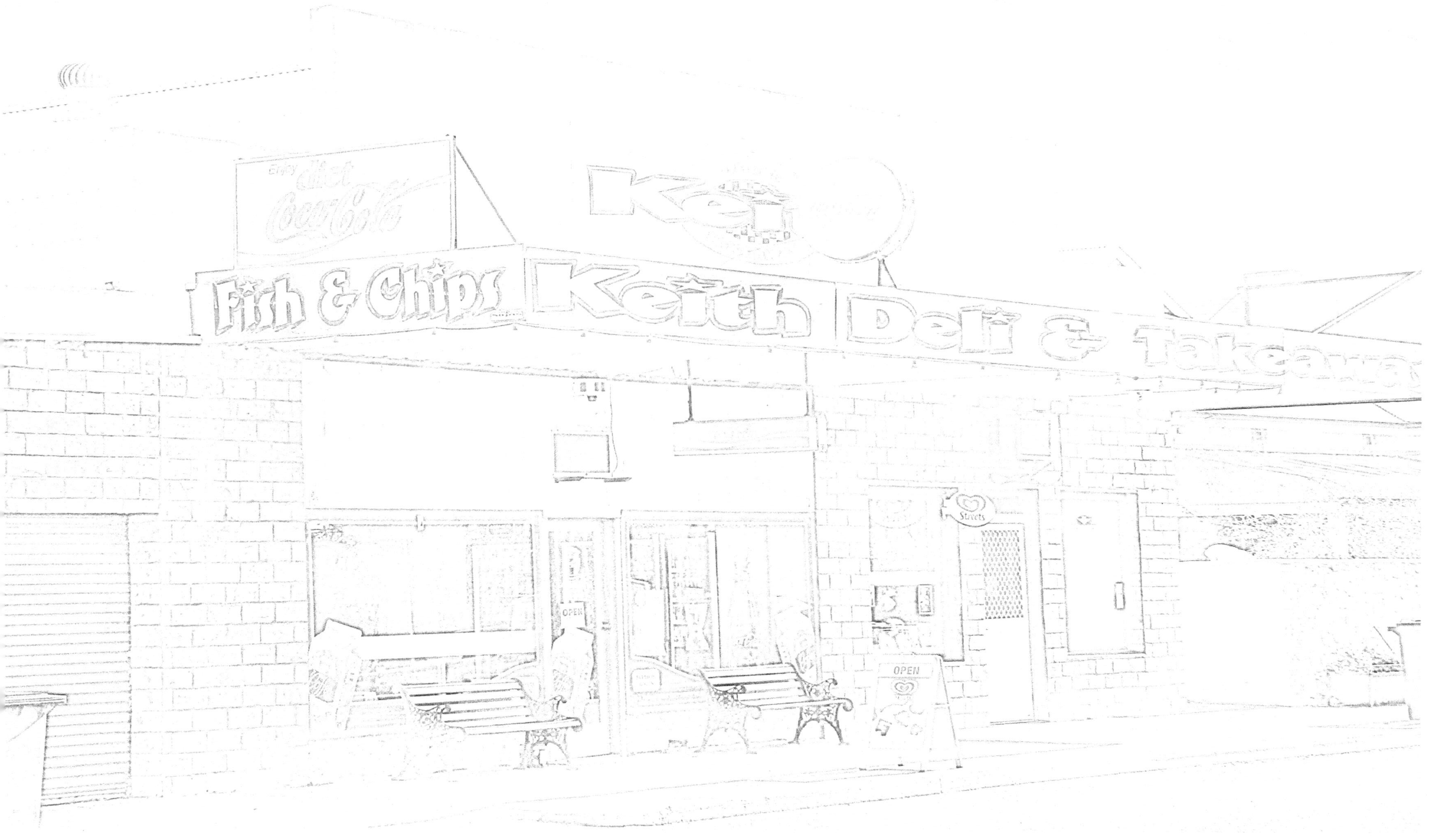
Enjoy diet Coca-Cola
Fish & Chips
Keith
Deli &
OPEN
Streets
OPEN

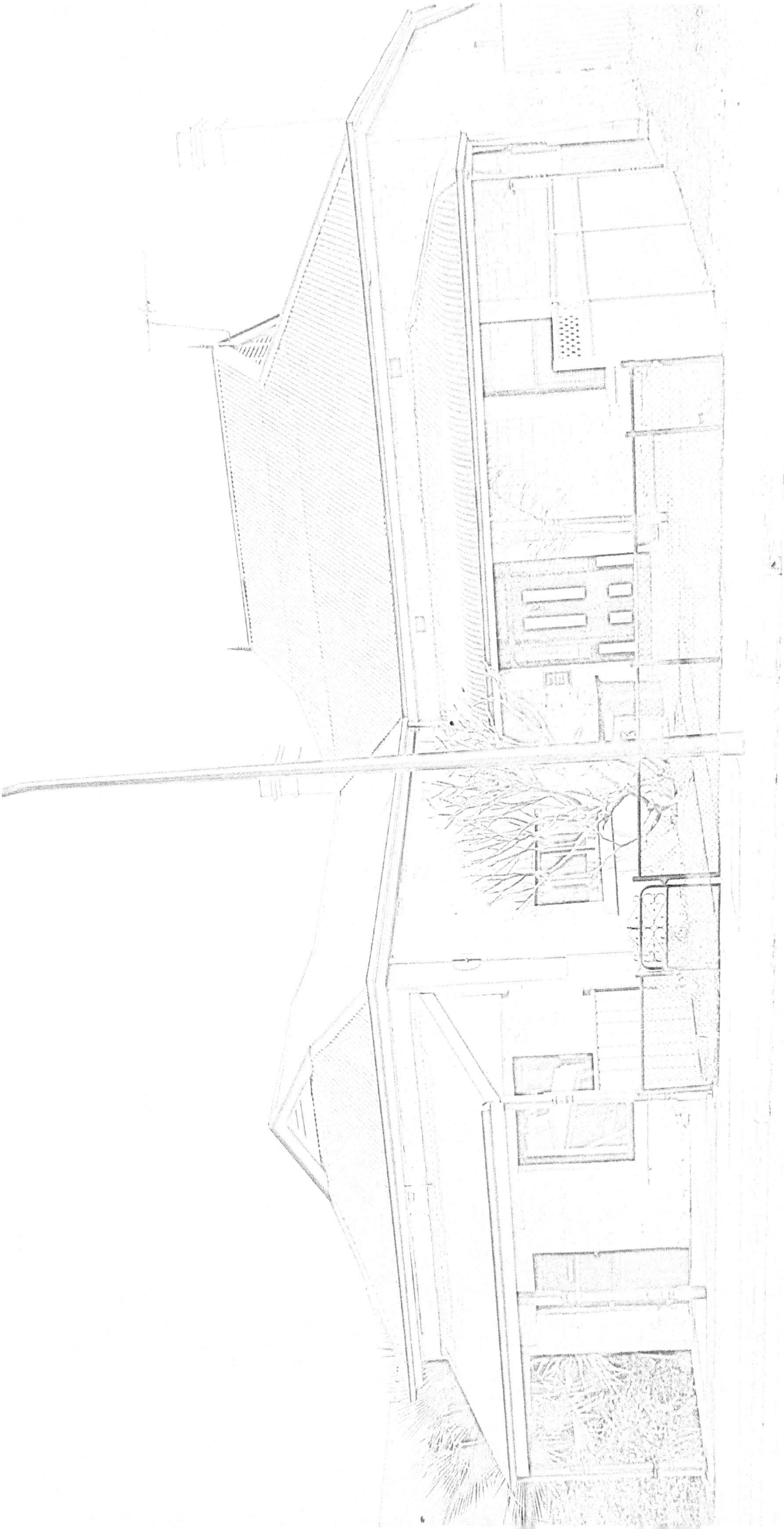

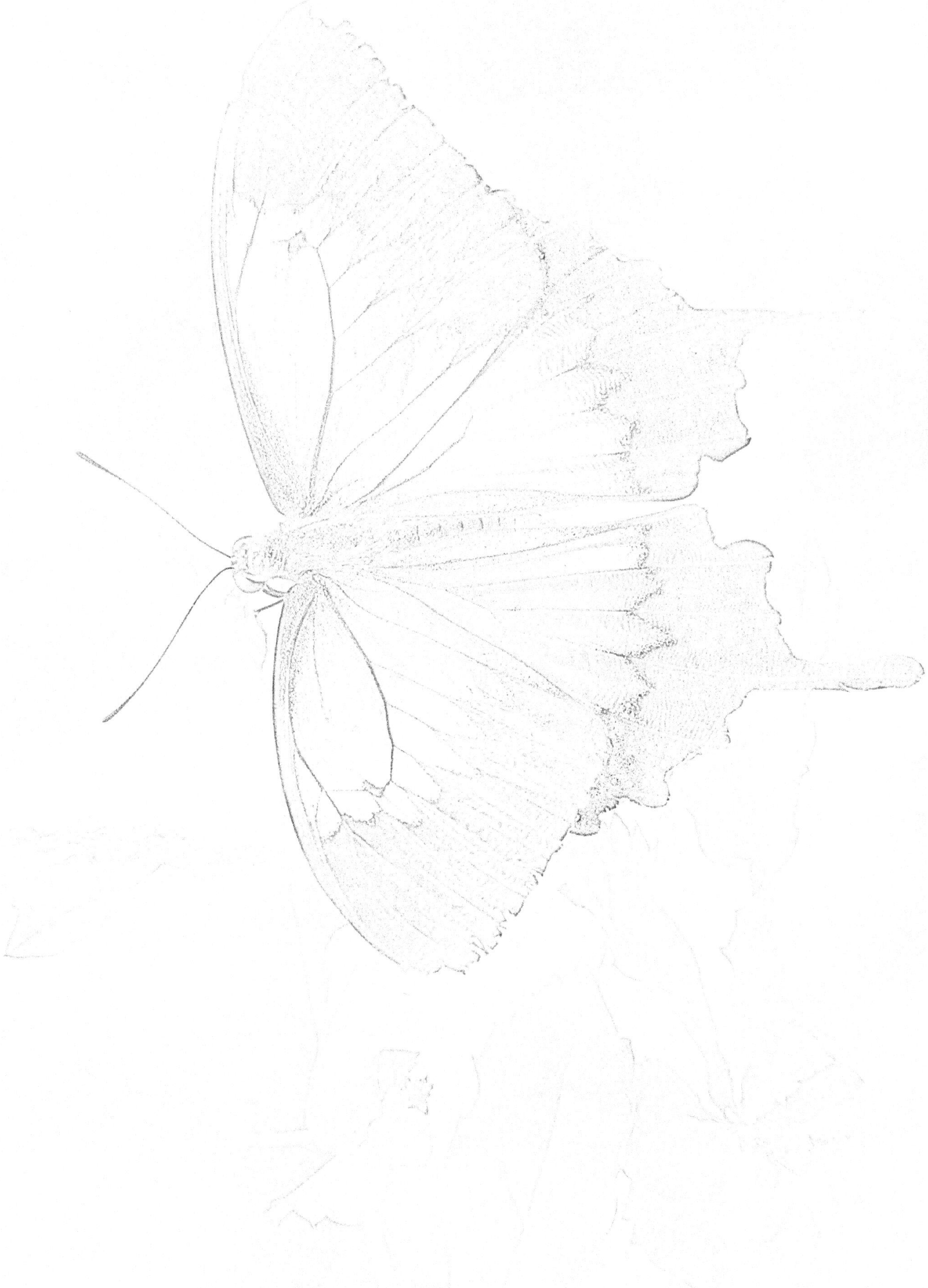

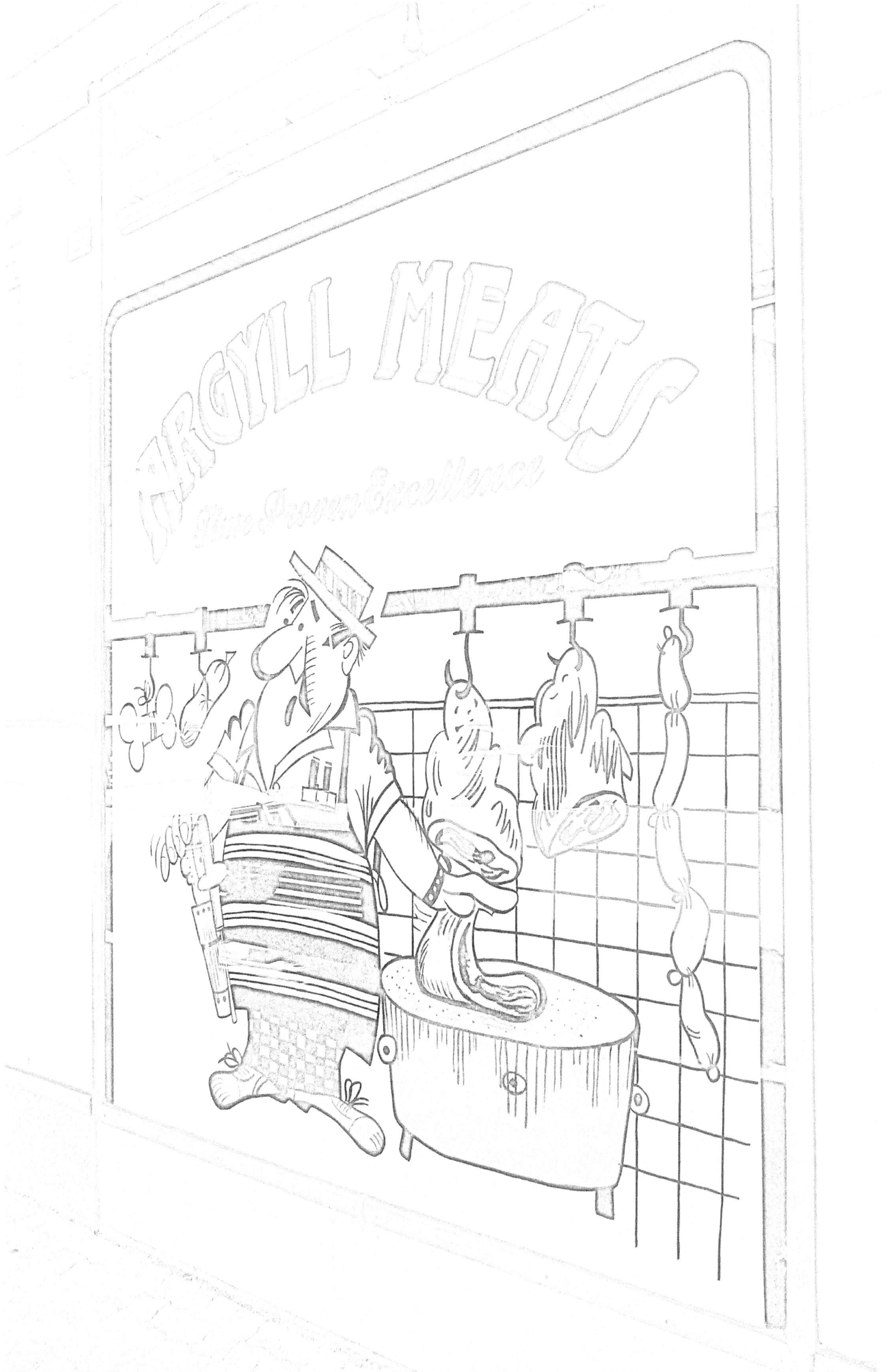
ARGYLL MEATS
Time Proven Excellence

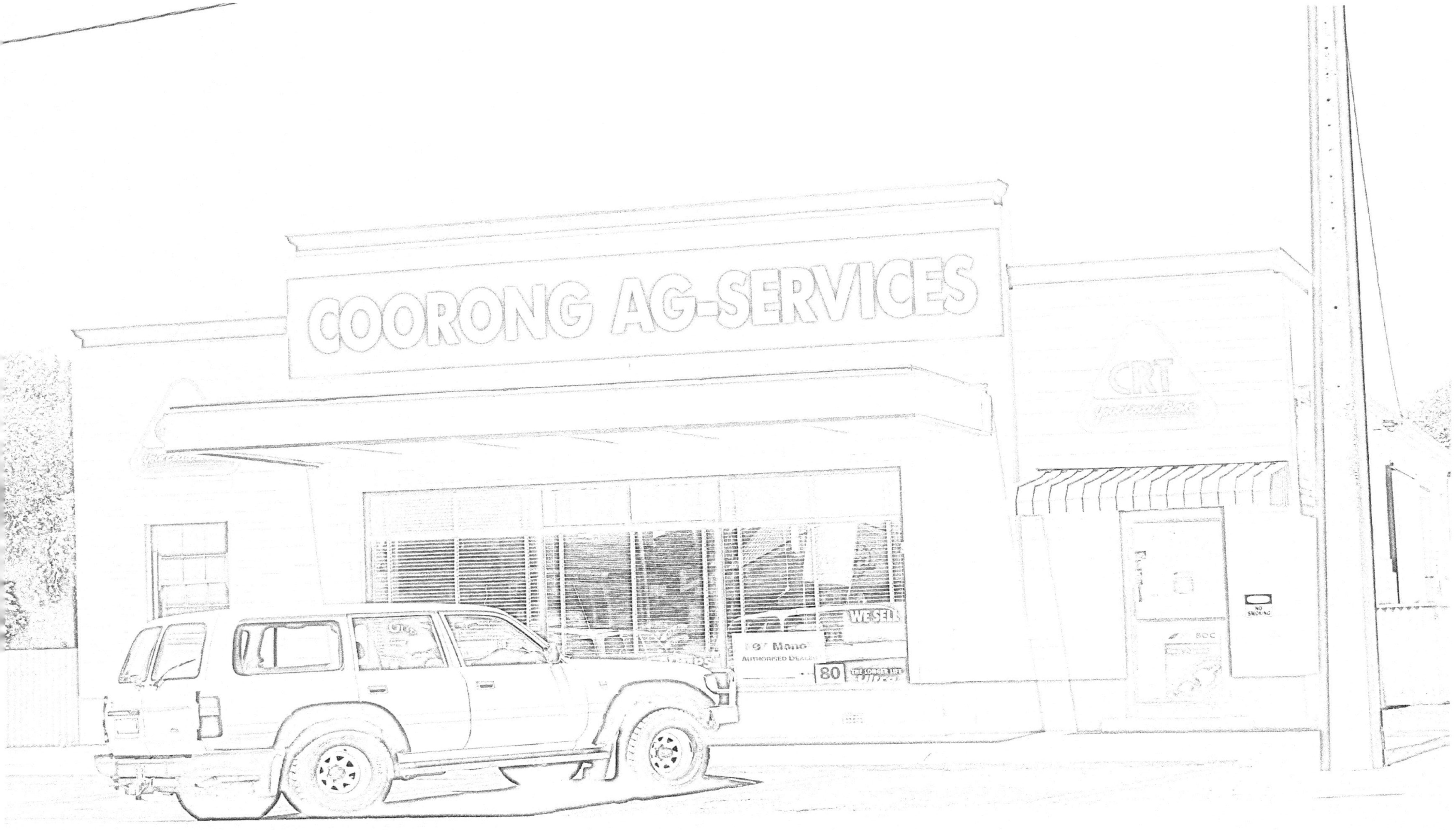
COORONG AG-SERVICES
CRT
WE SELL
AUTHORISED DEALER
80
NO SMOKING
BOC

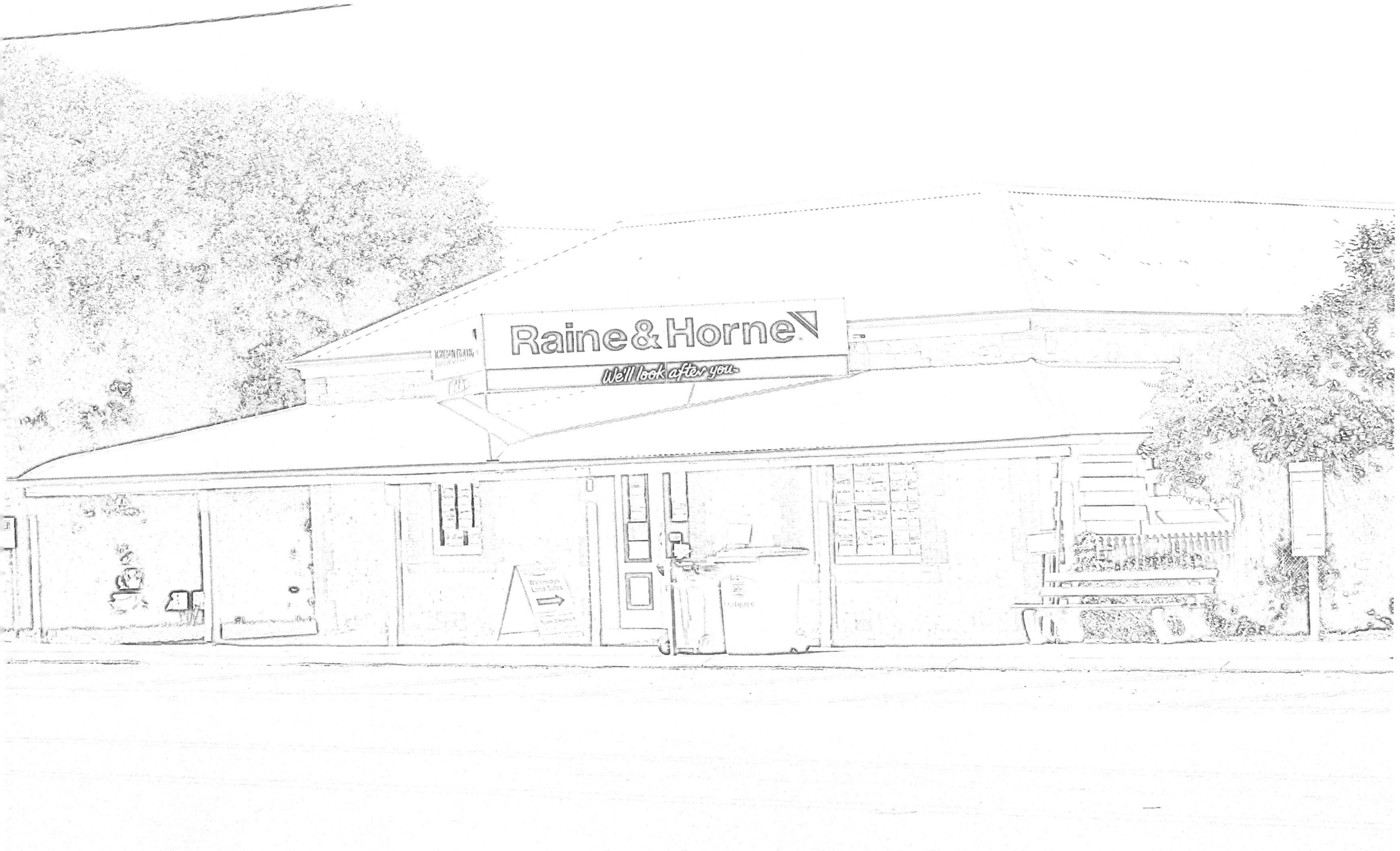
Raine&Horne
We'll look after you.

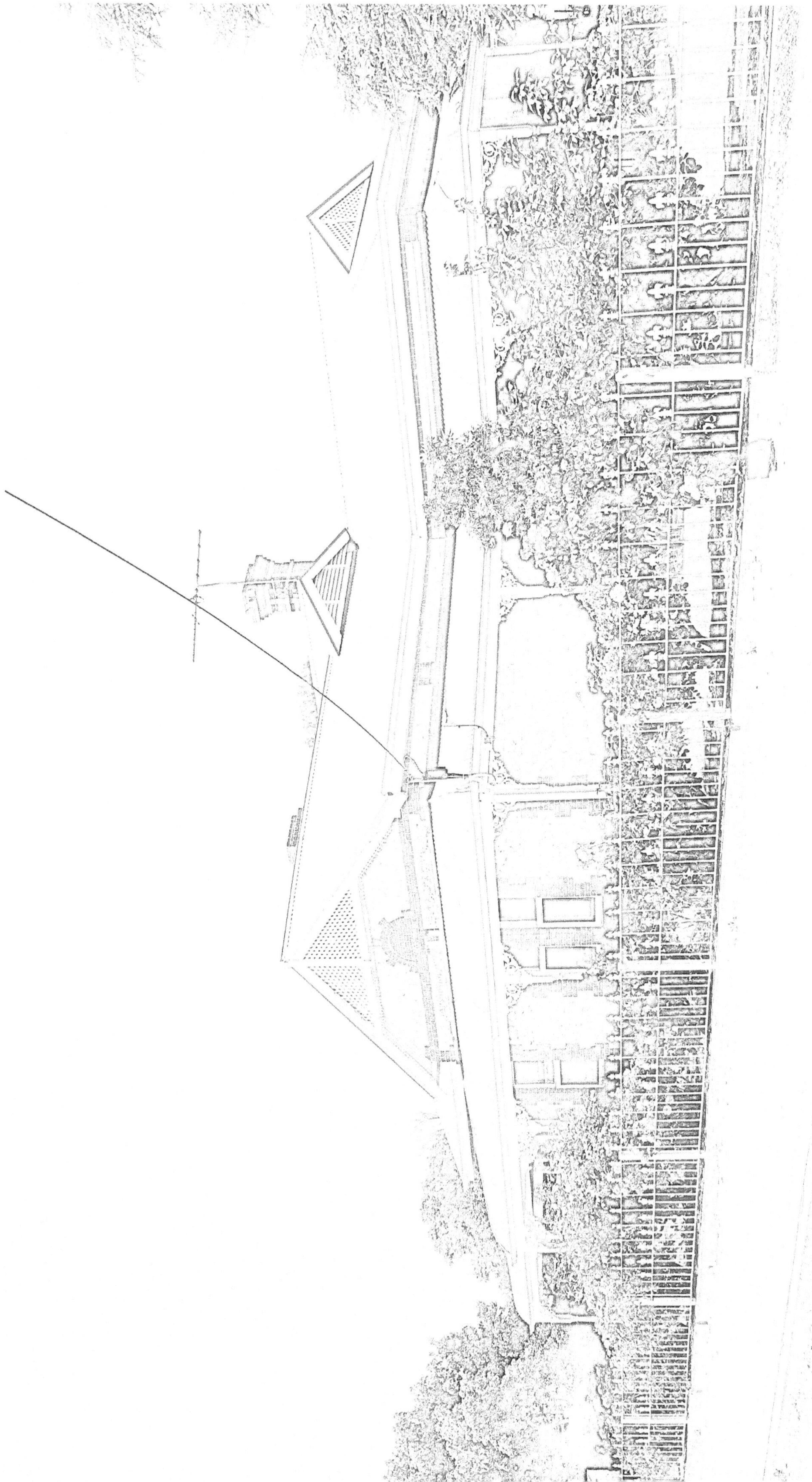

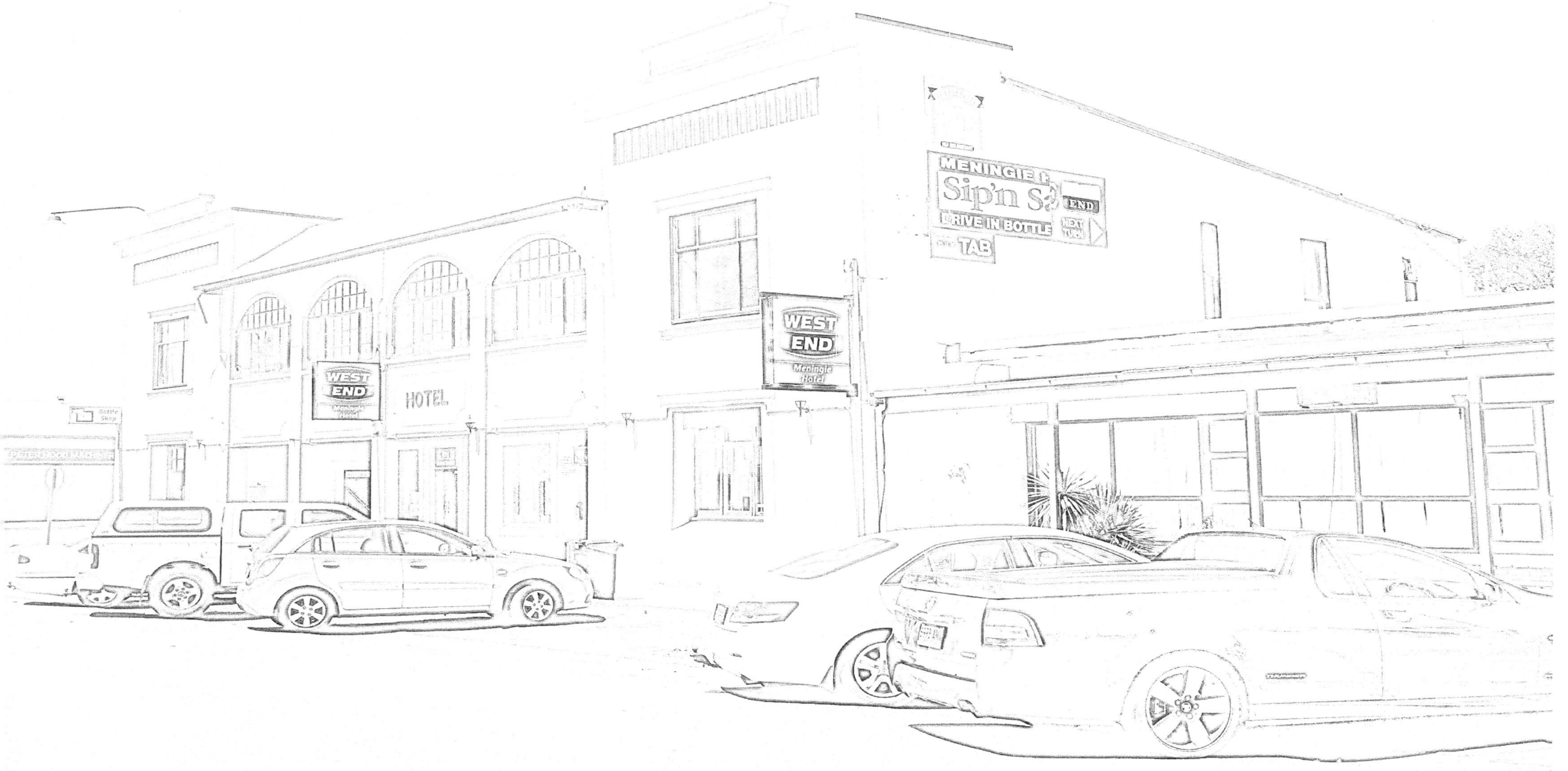
HOTEL
WEST END
WEST END
Meningie Hotel
MENINGIE
Sip'n S
END
DRIVE IN BOTTLE
NEXT TURN
TAB

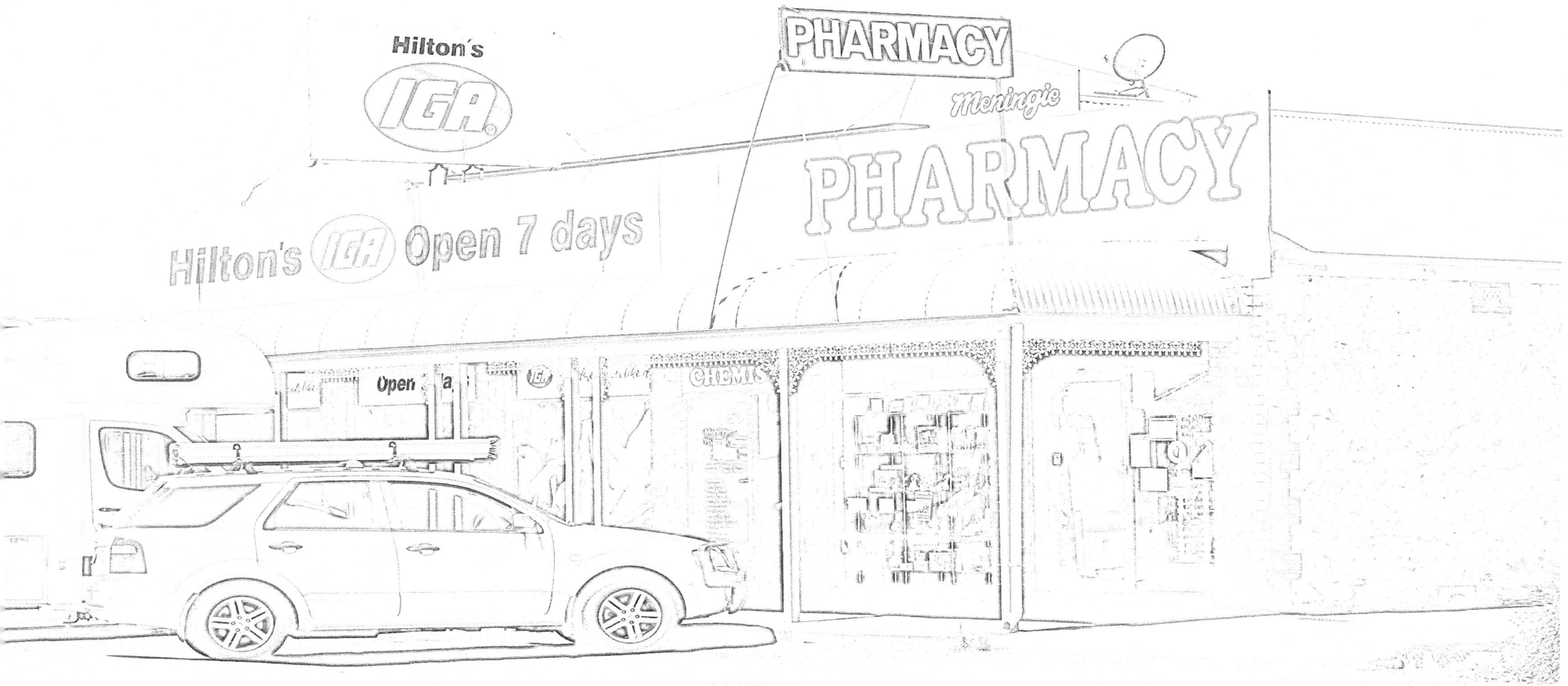
Hilton's
IGA
PHARMACY
Meningie
PHARMACY
Hilton's IGA Open 7 days
Open
CHEMIS

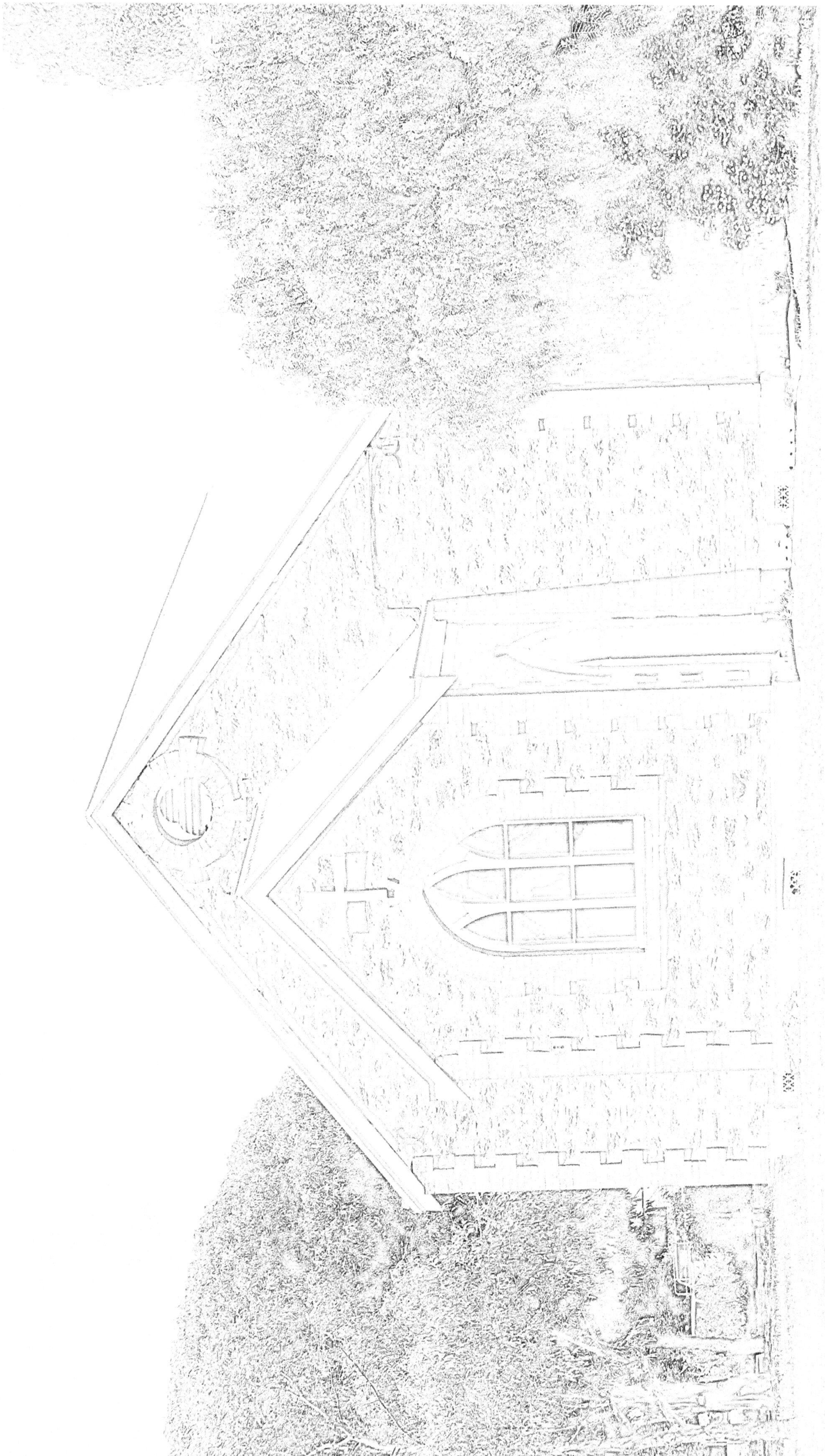

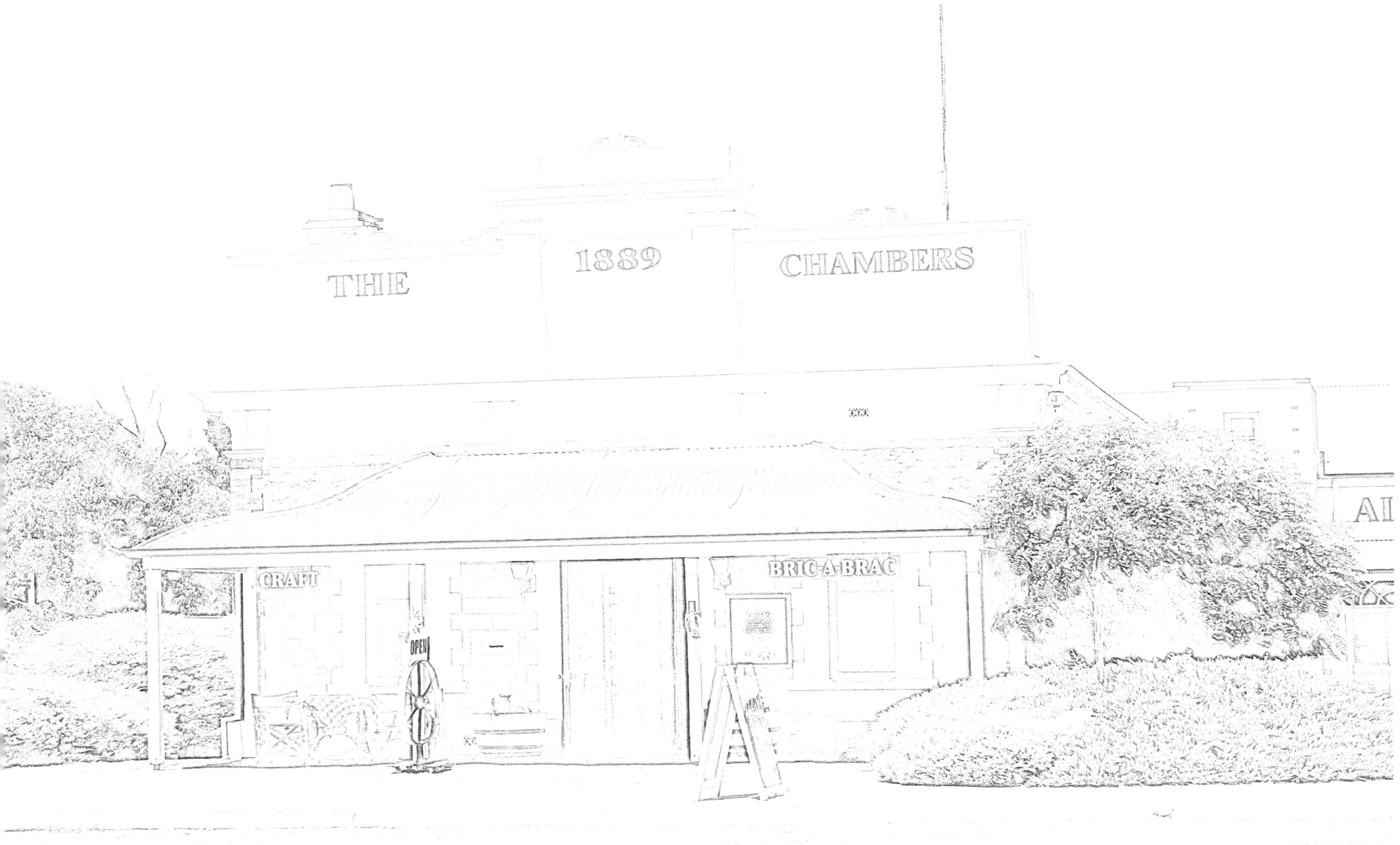
THE
1889
CHAMBERS
CRAFT
OPEN
BRIC-A-BRAC

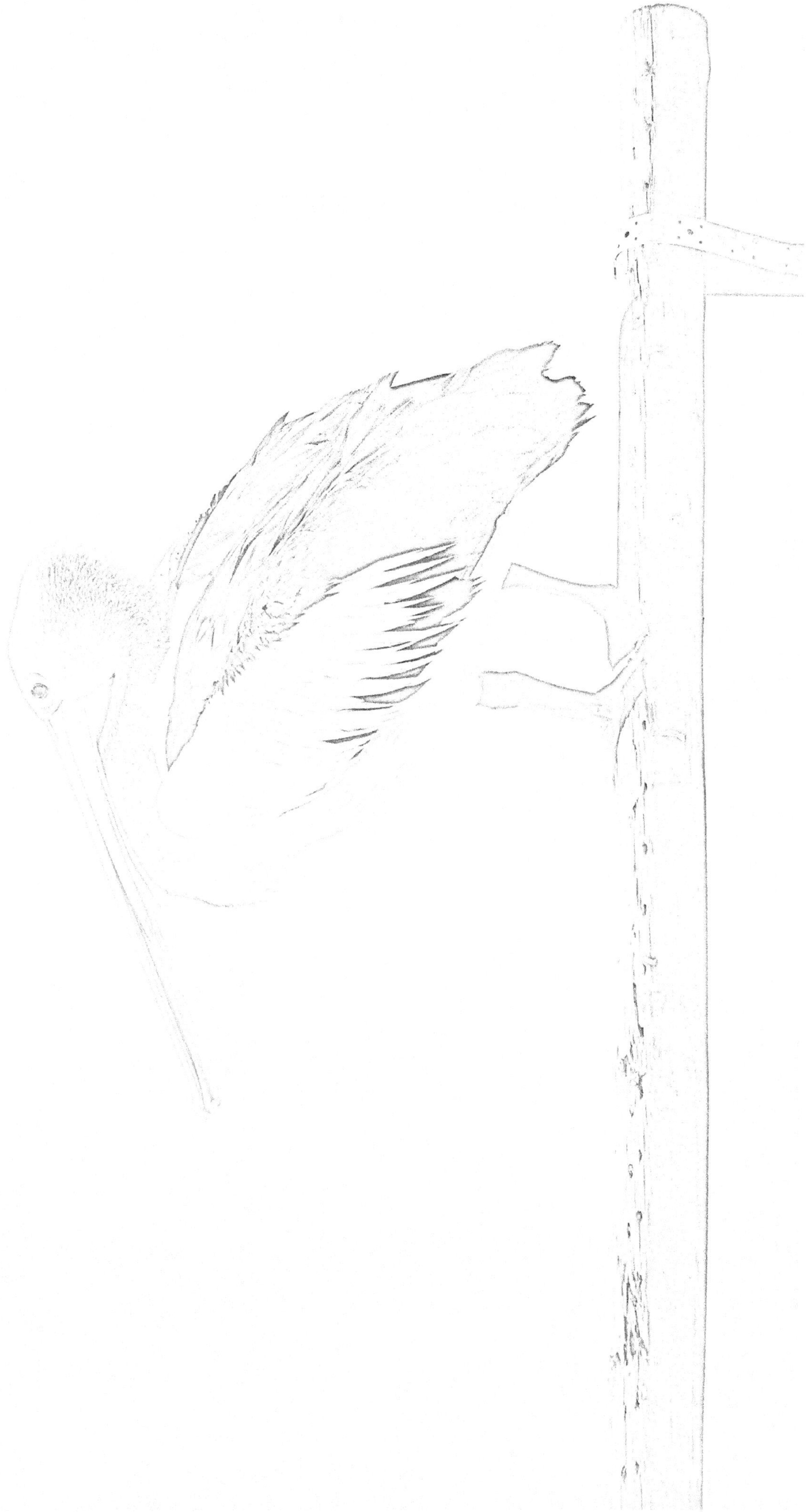

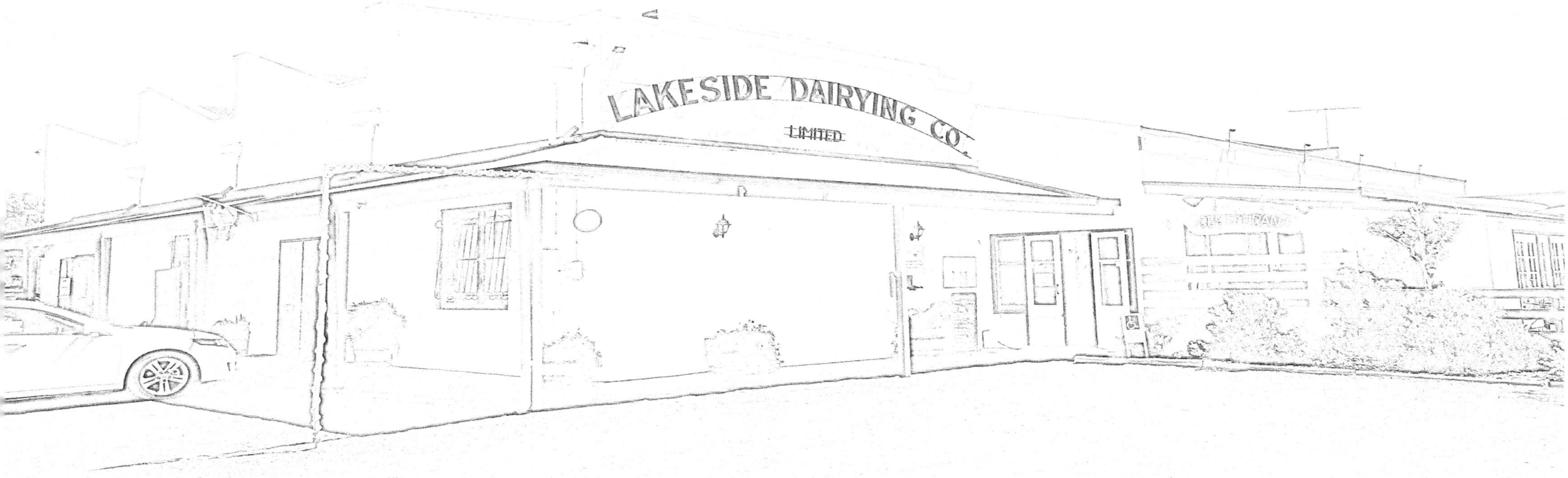
LAKESIDE DAIRYING CO.
LIMITED

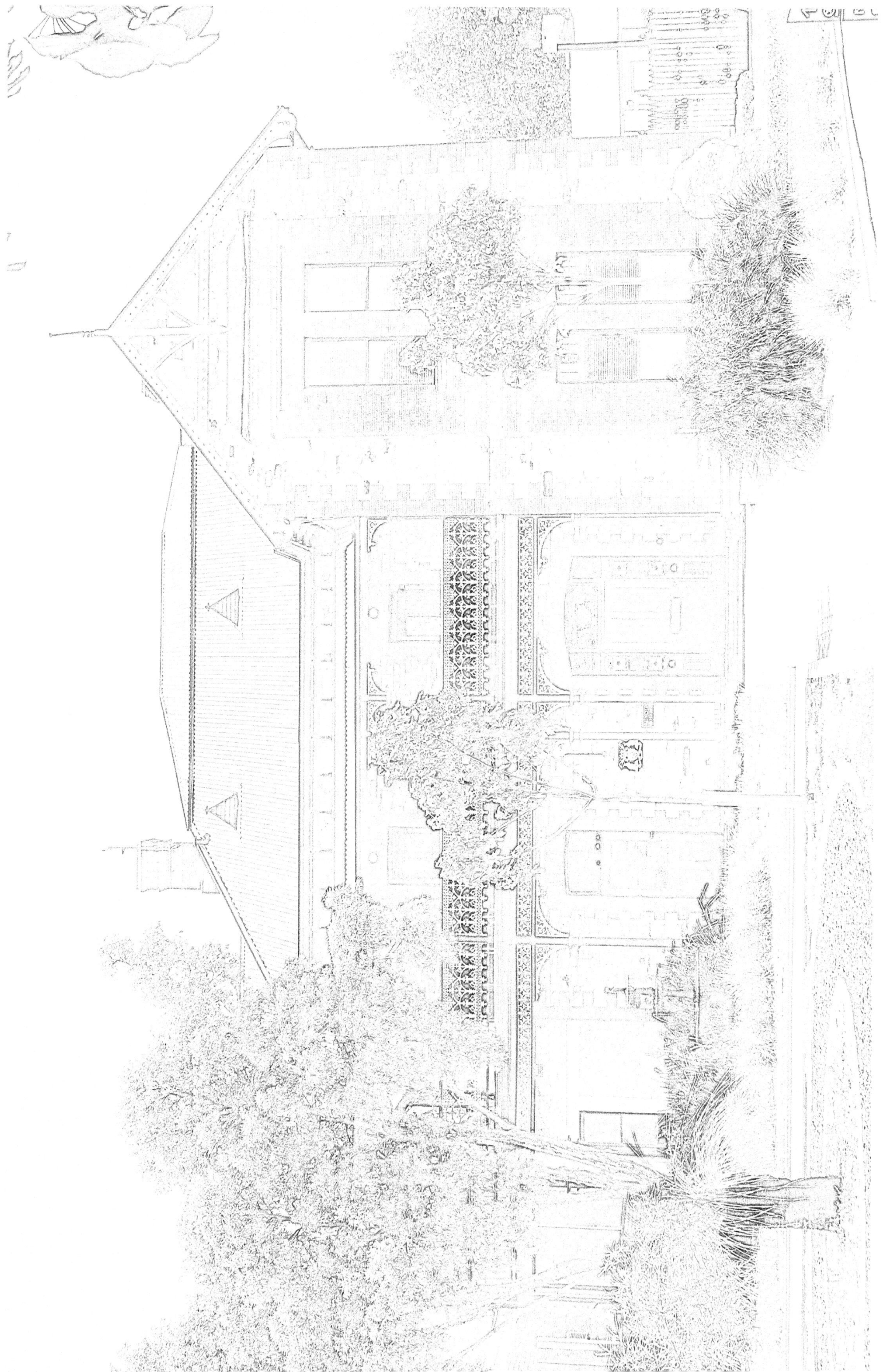

LAND CRUISER
CRIKEY

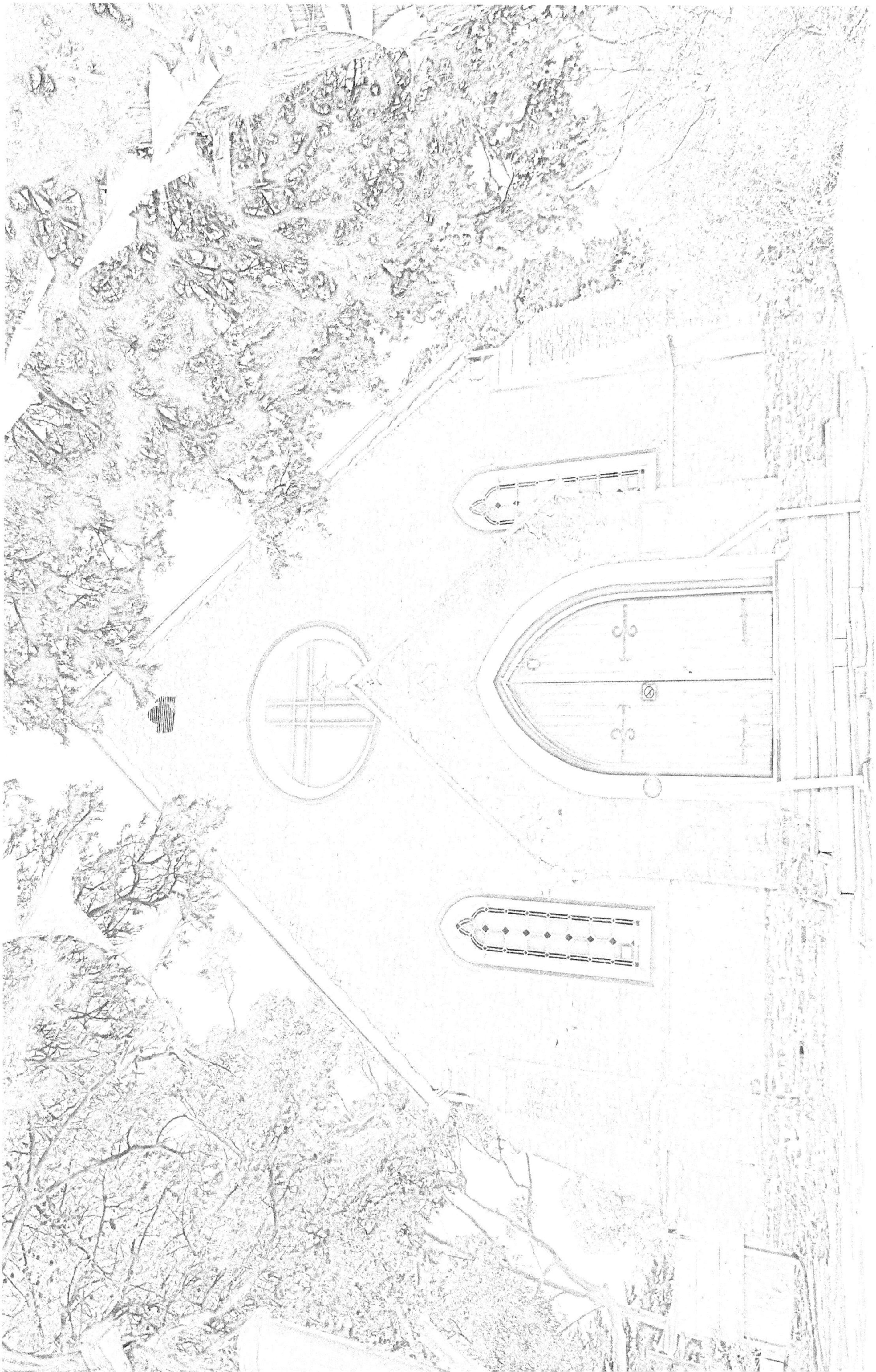

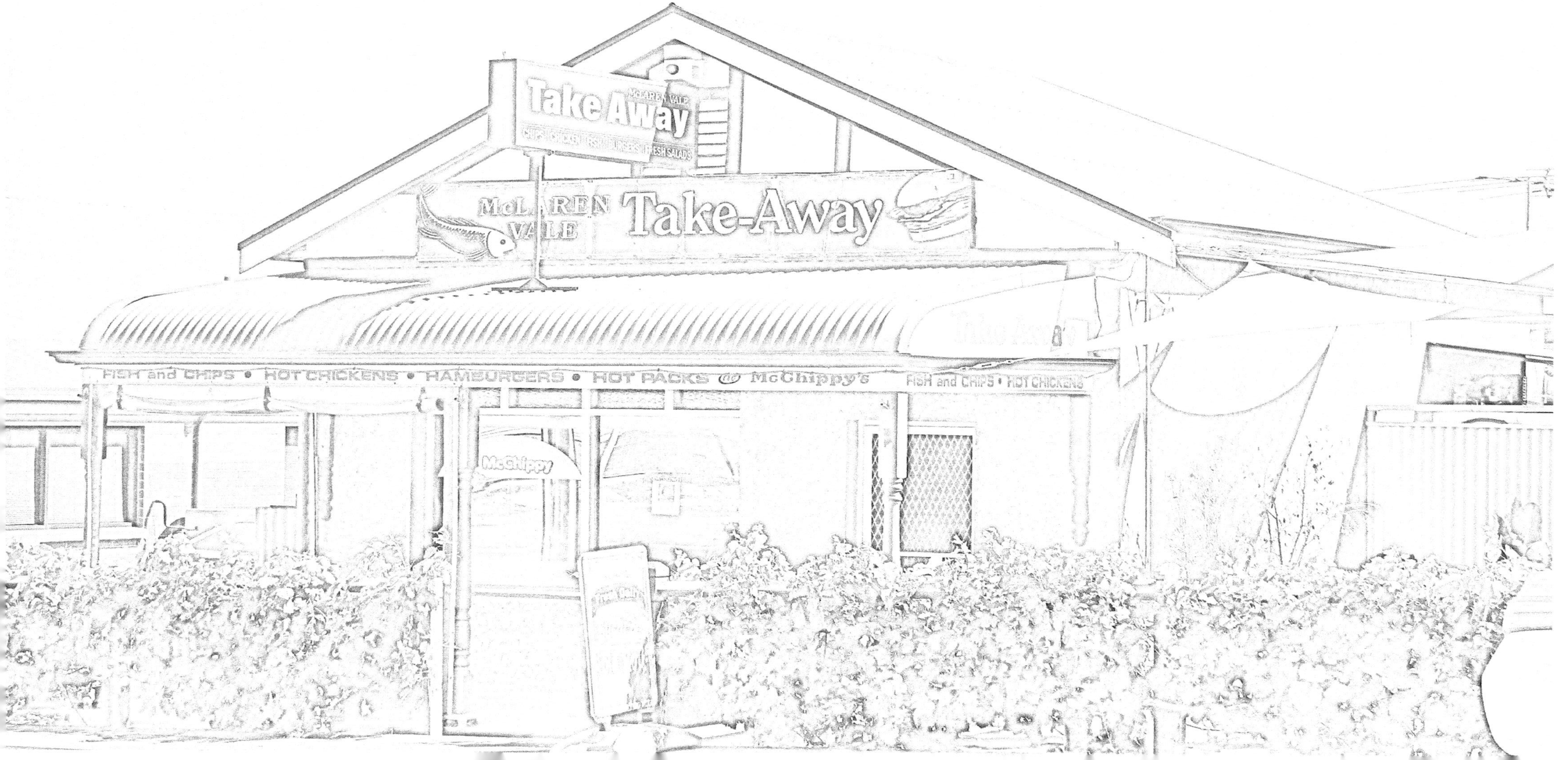
Take Away
McLAREN VALE
CHIPS CHICKEN FISH BURGERS FRESH SALADS
McLAREN VALE
Take-Away
FISH and CHIPS • HOT CHICKENS • HAMBURGERS • HOT PACKS @ McChippy's
FISH and CHIPS • HOT CHICKENS
McChippy

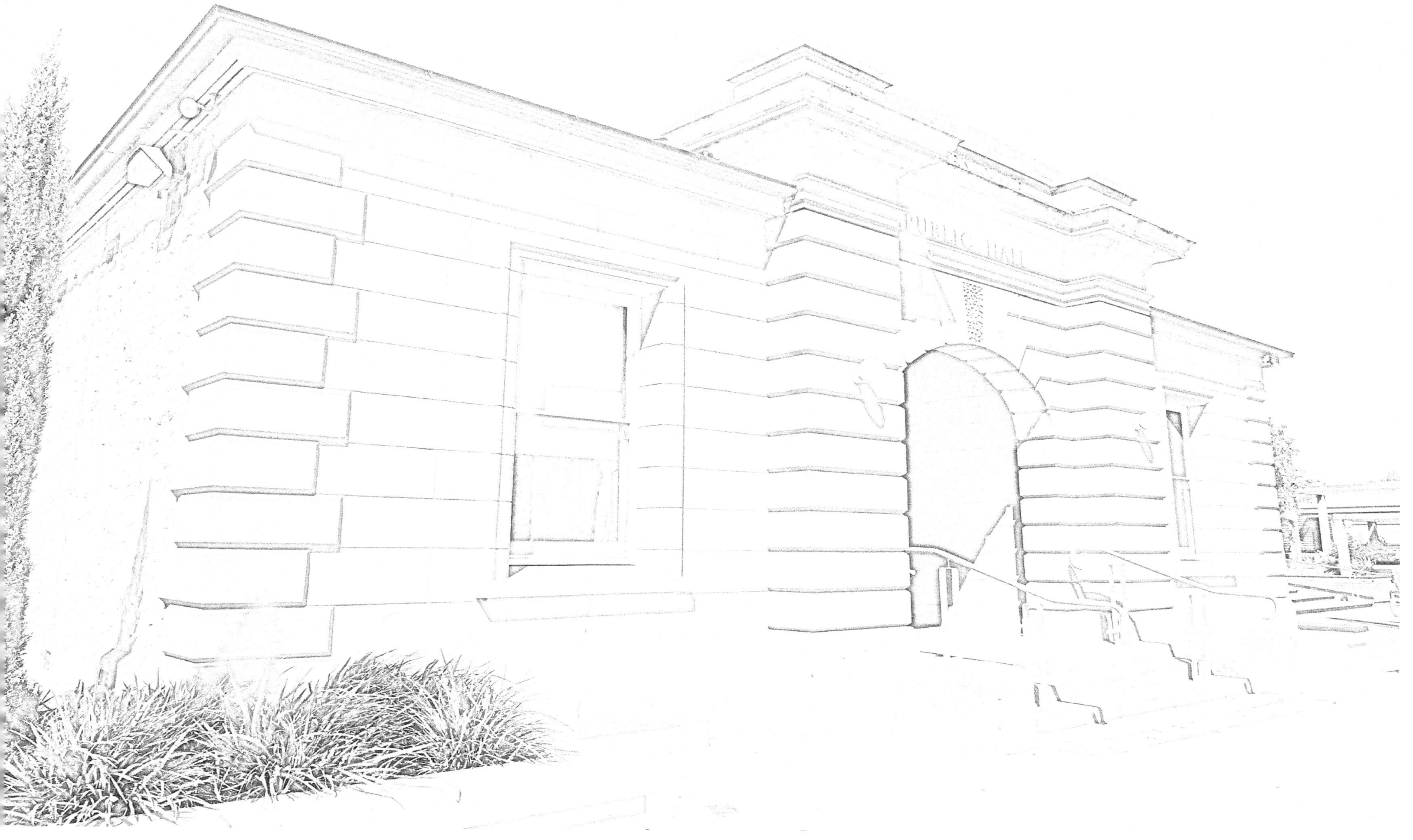
PUBLIC HALL

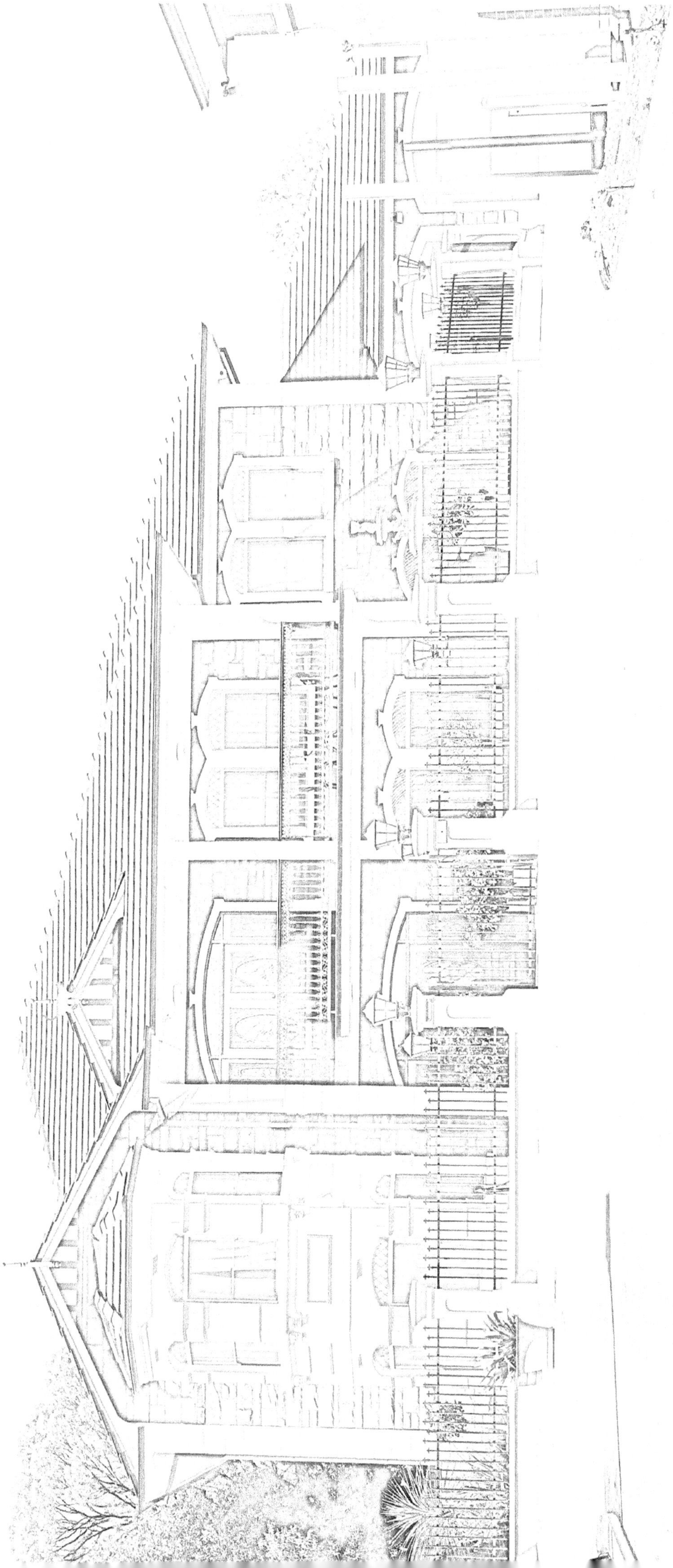

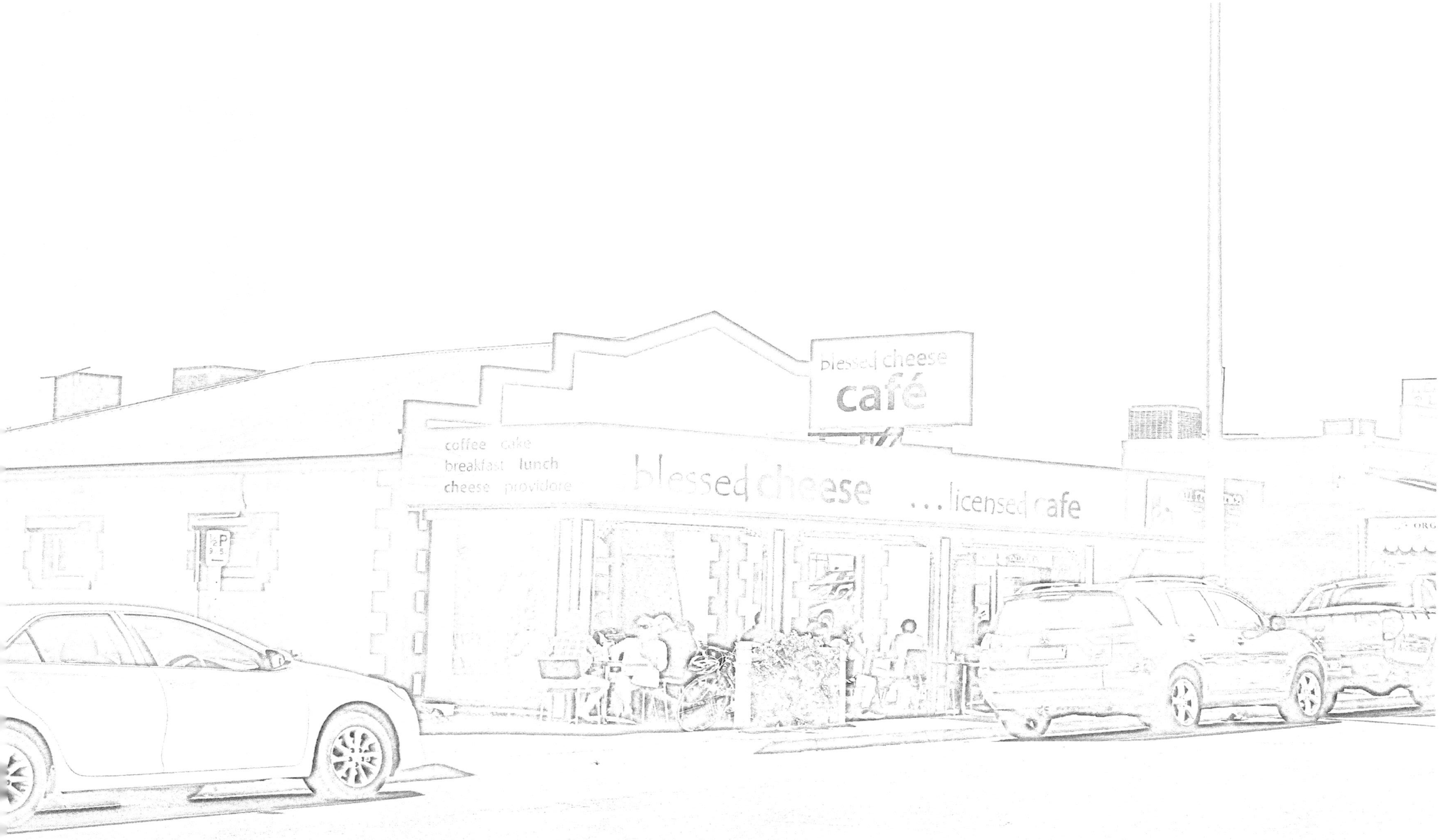
blessed cheese
café
coffee cake
breakfast lunch
cheese providore
blessed cheese
...licensed cafe

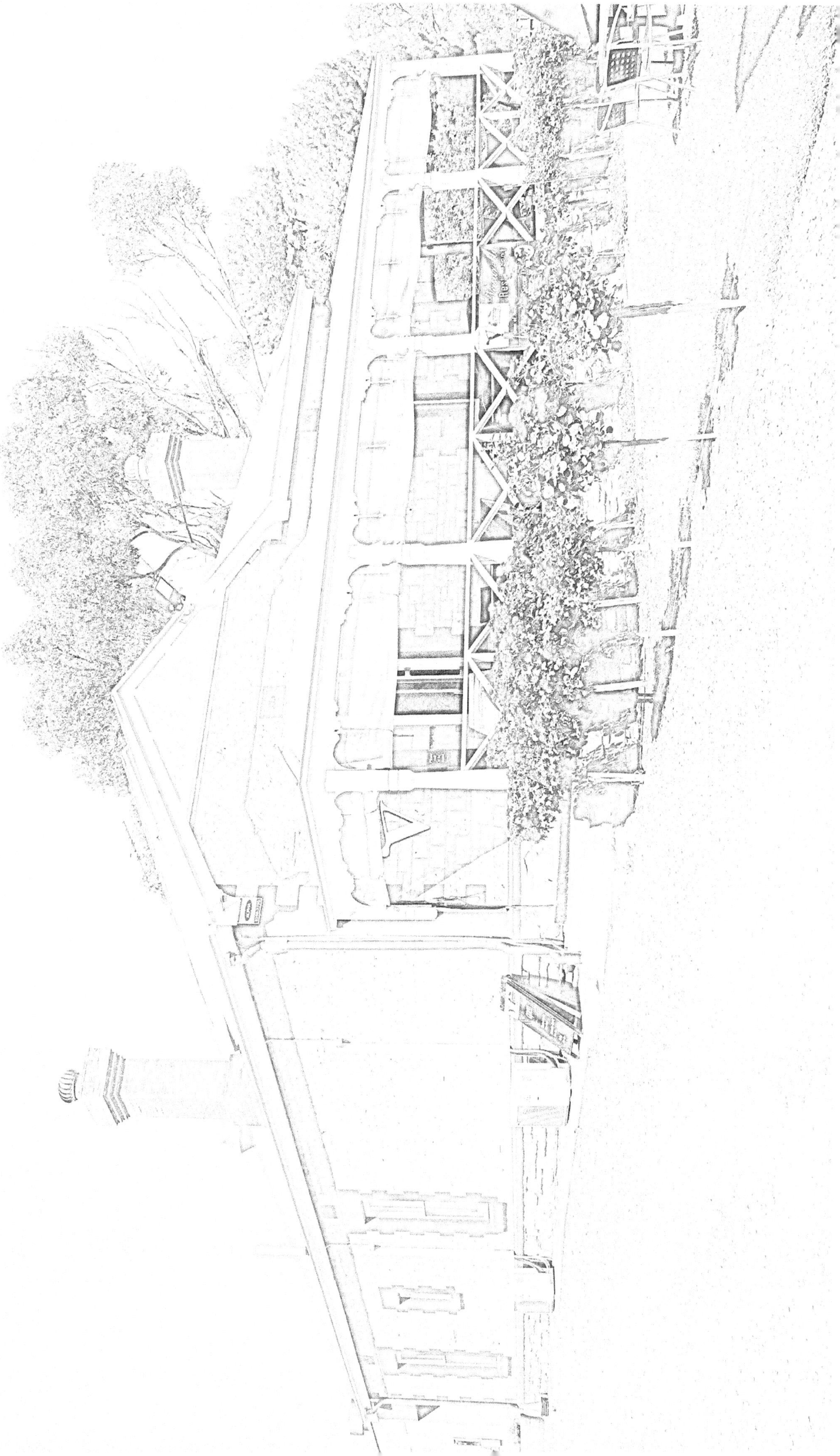

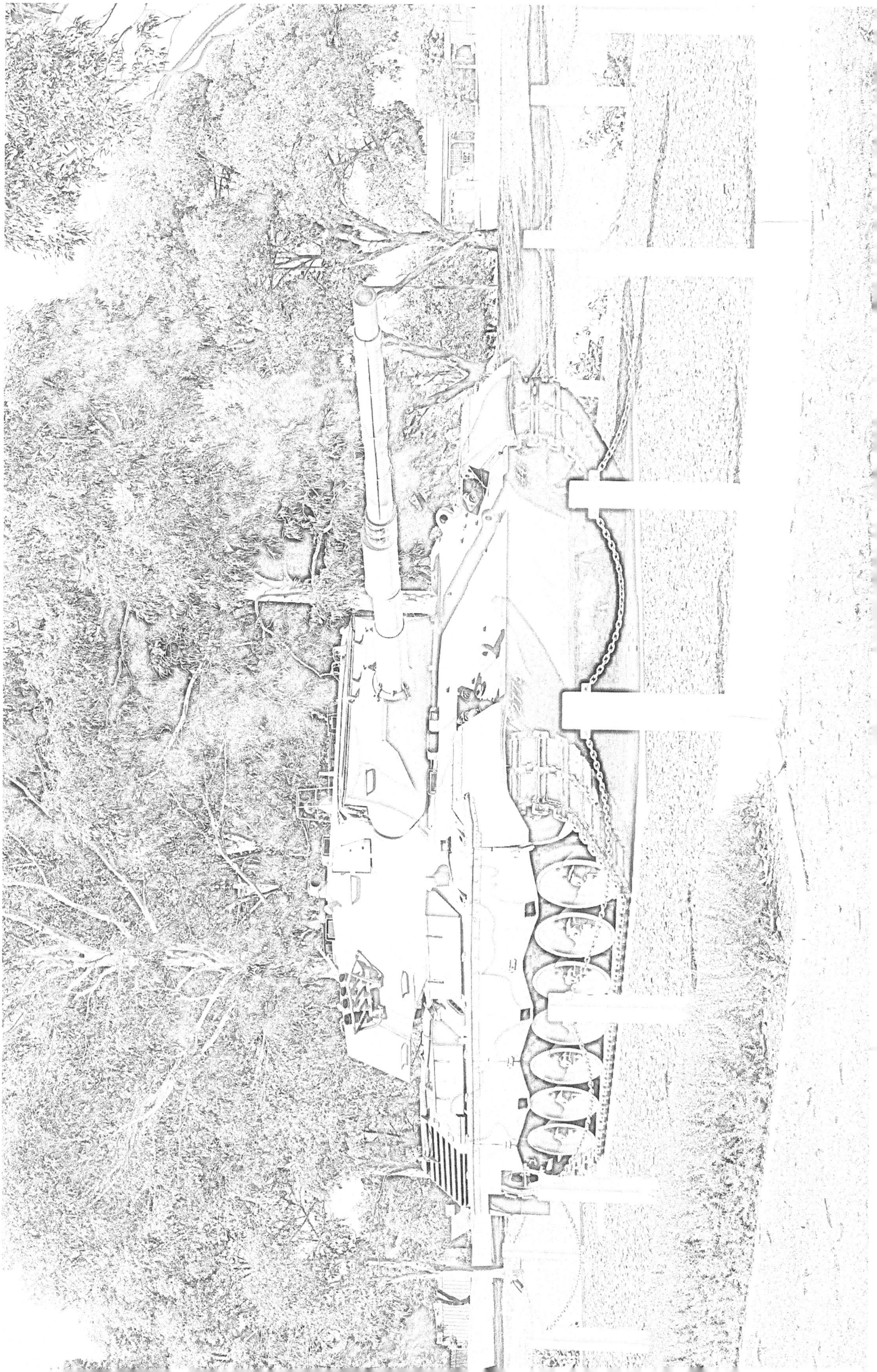

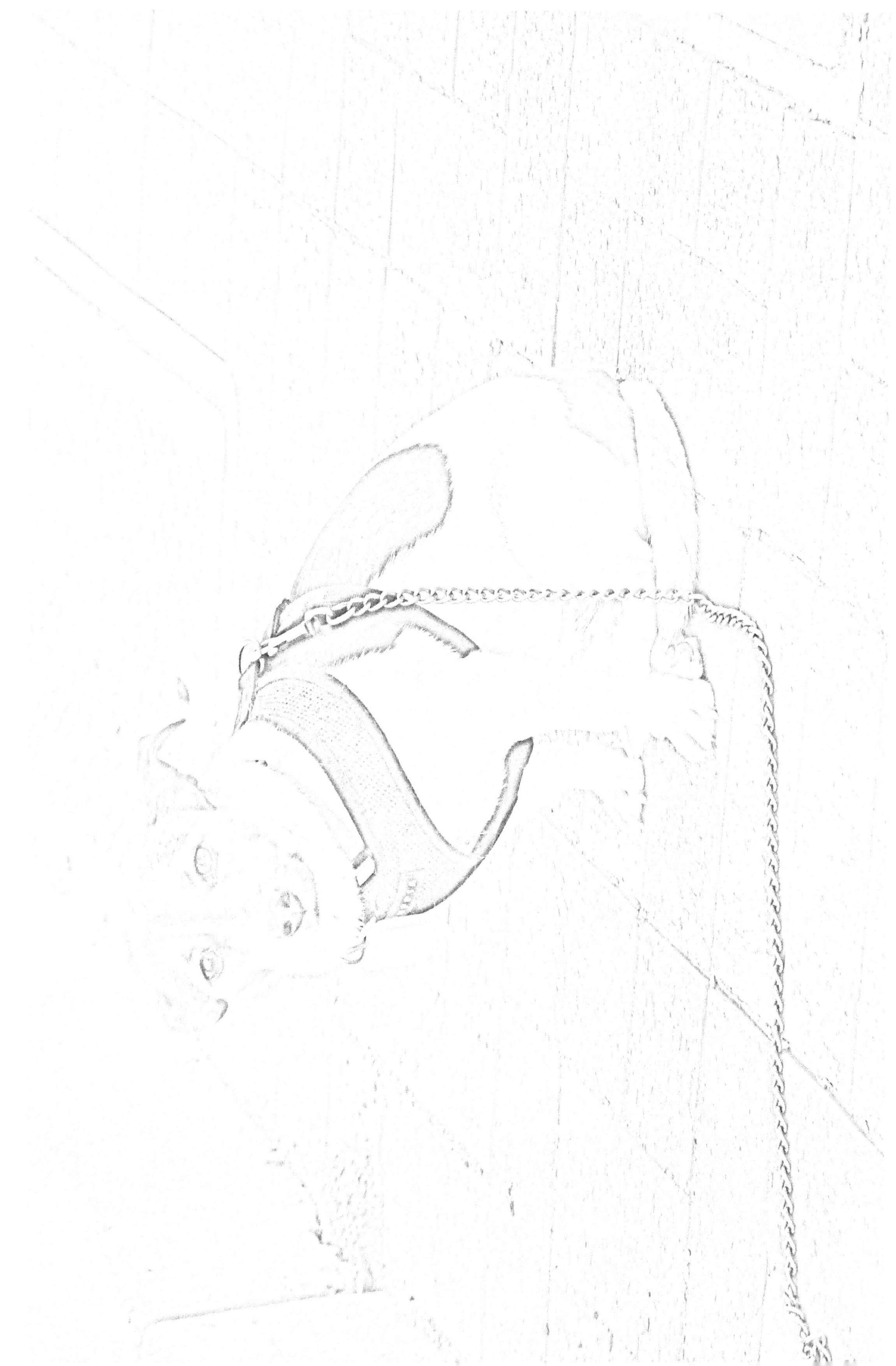

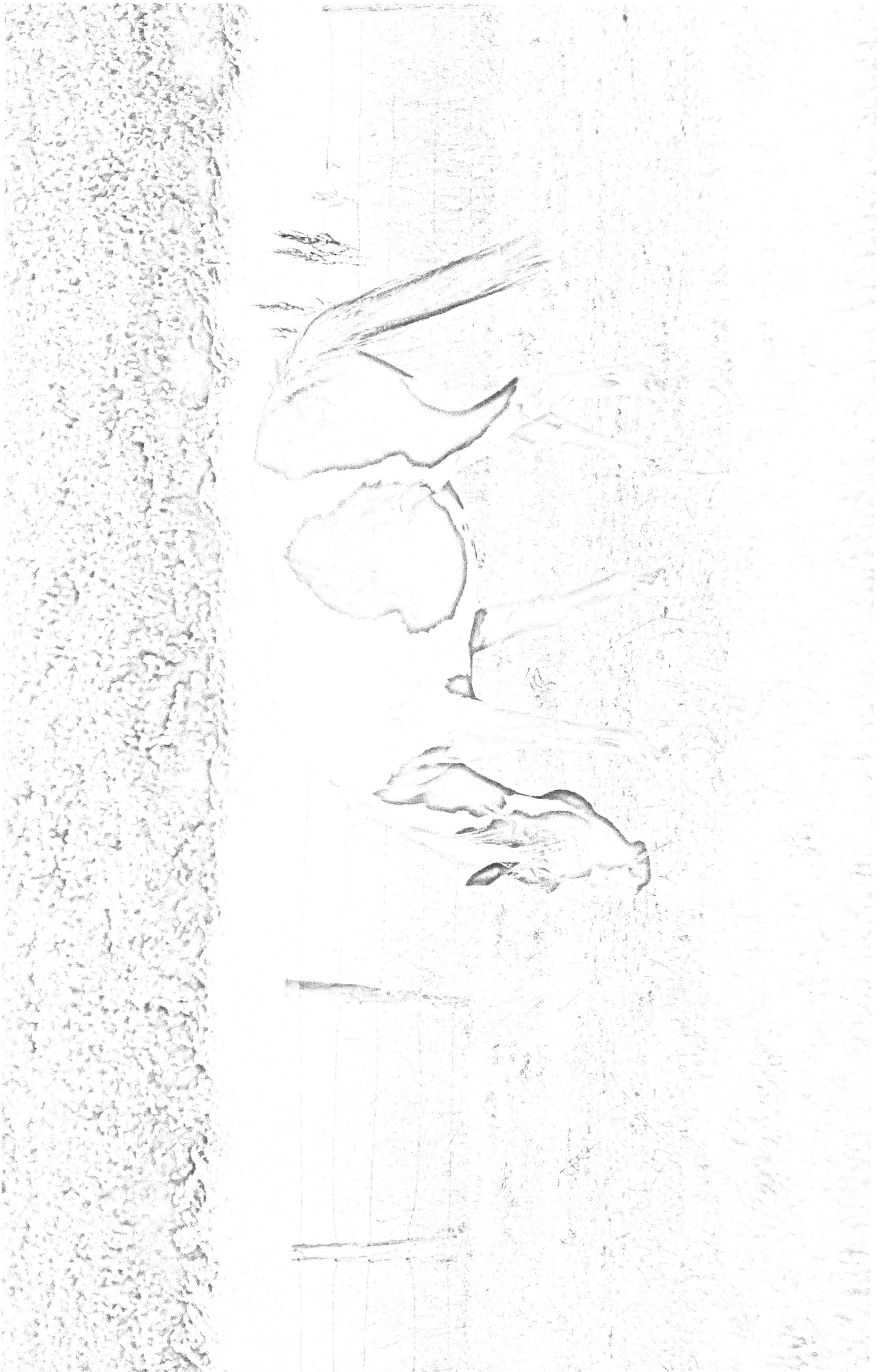

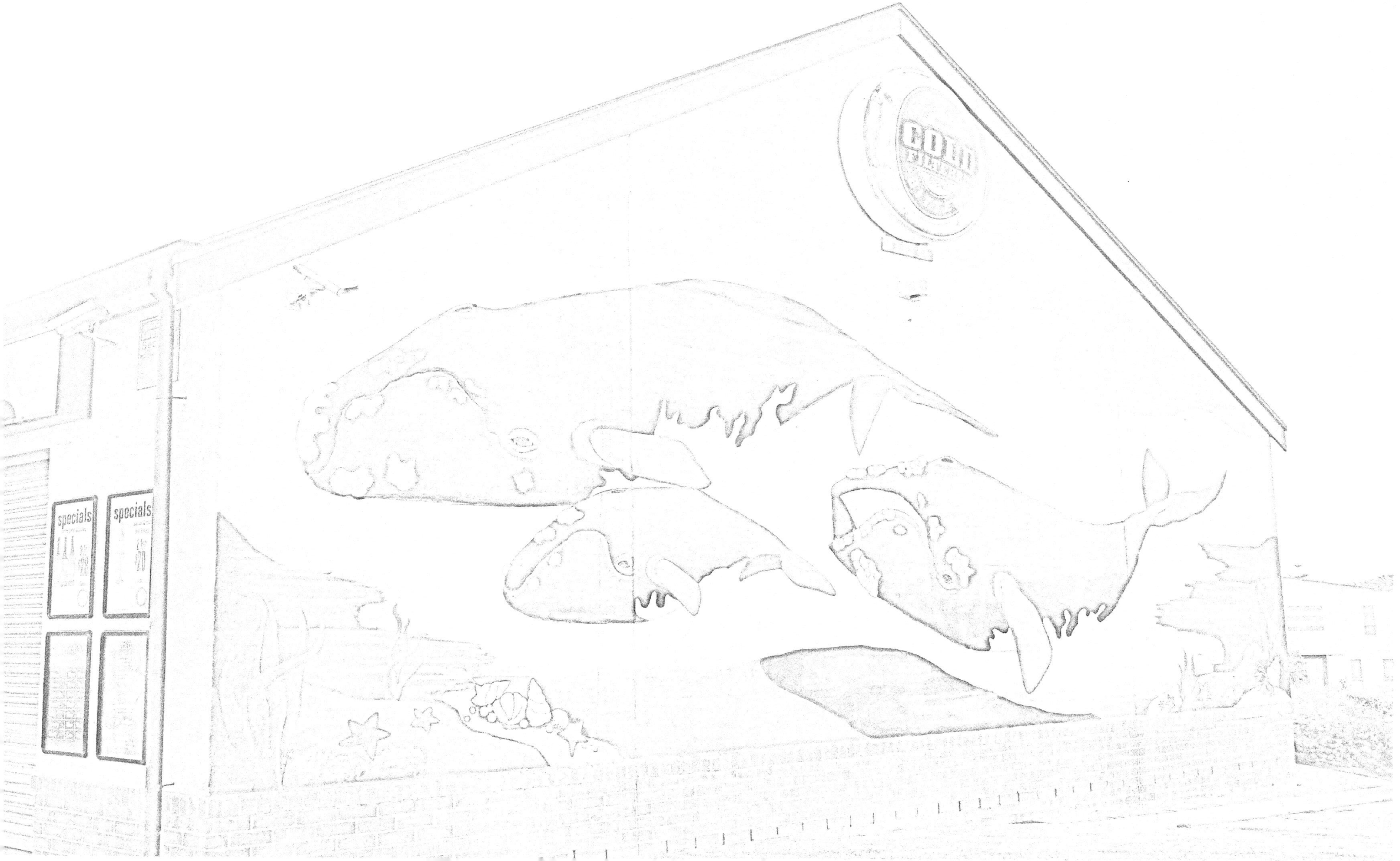
specials
specials

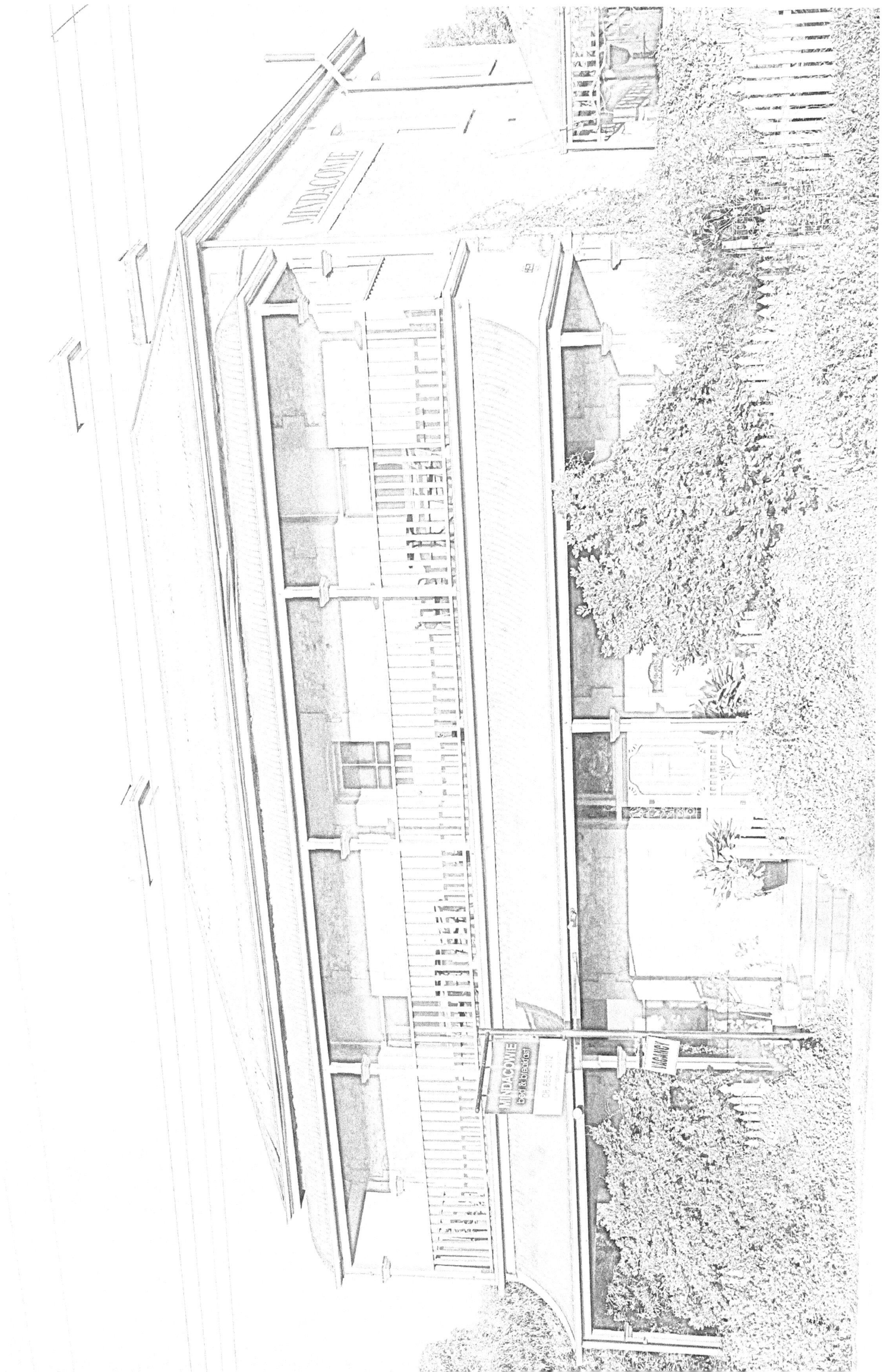
MINDACOWIE
MINDACOWIE
bed & breakfast

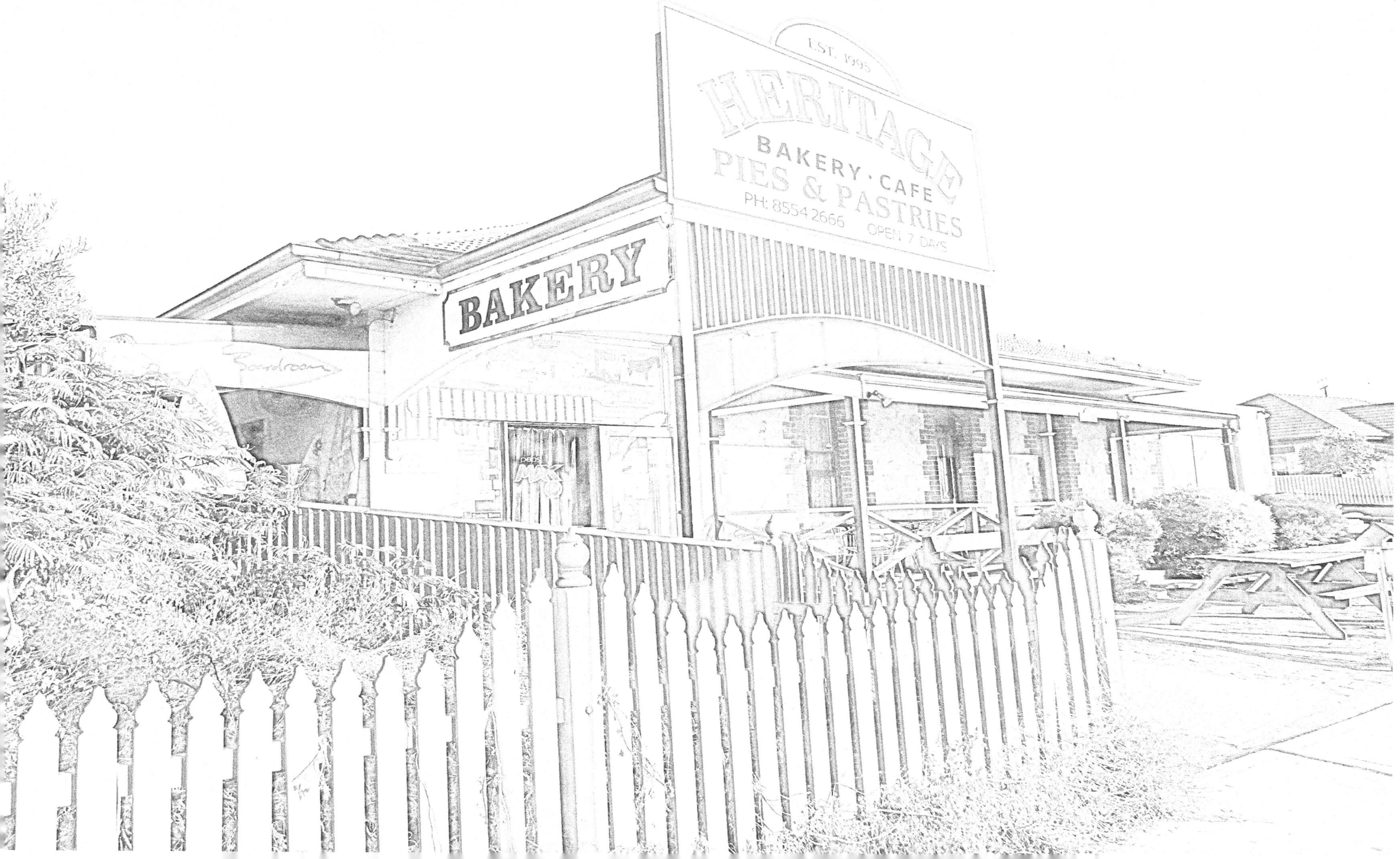
EST. 1995
HERITAGE
BAKERY · CAFE
PIES & PASTRIES
PH: 8554 2666
OPEN 7 DAYS
BAKERY

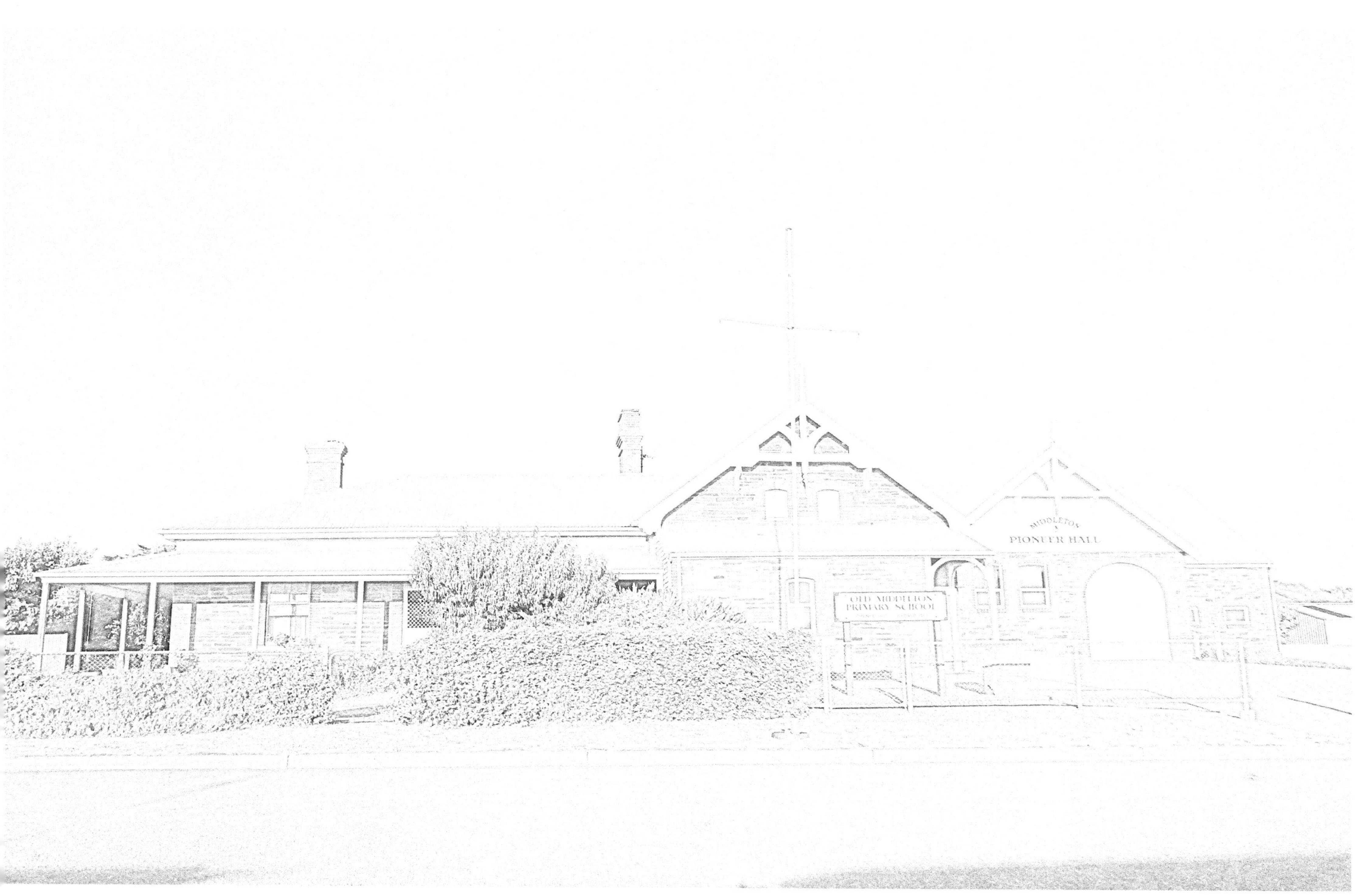
MIDDLETON
PIONEER HALL
OLD MIDDLETON
PRIMARY SCHOOL

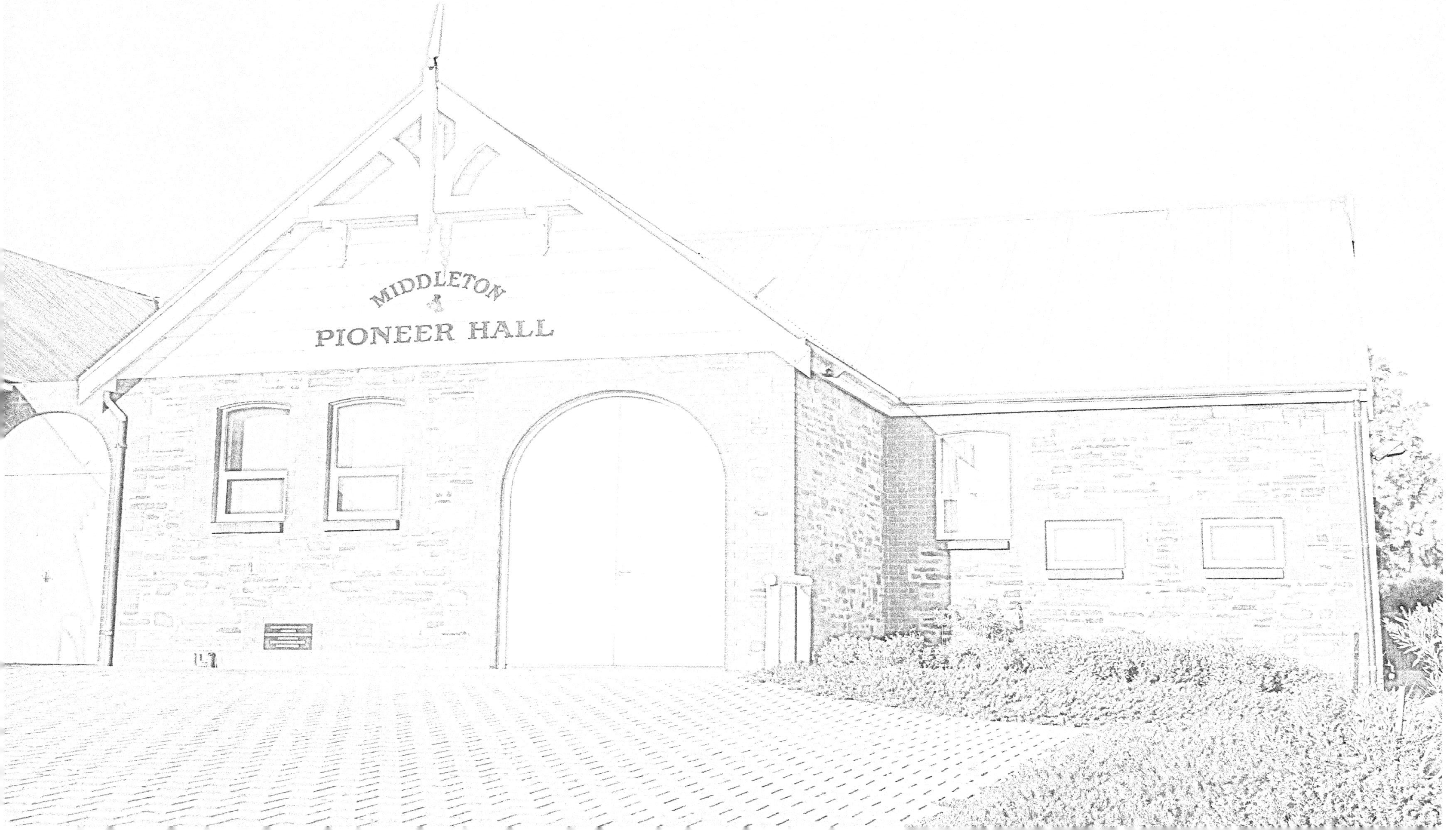
MIDDLETON
PIONEER HALL

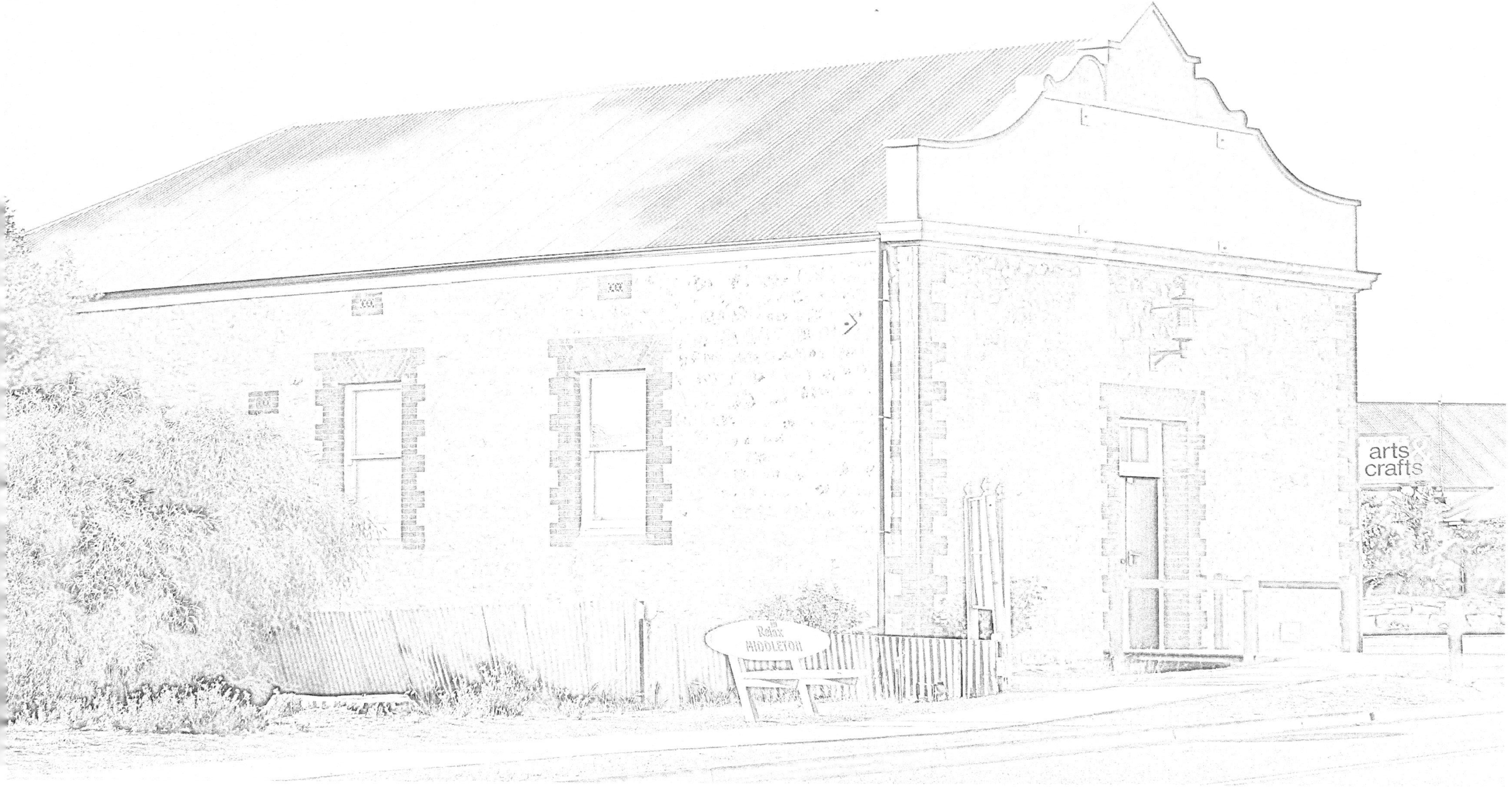
arts
crafts
Relax
MIDDLETON

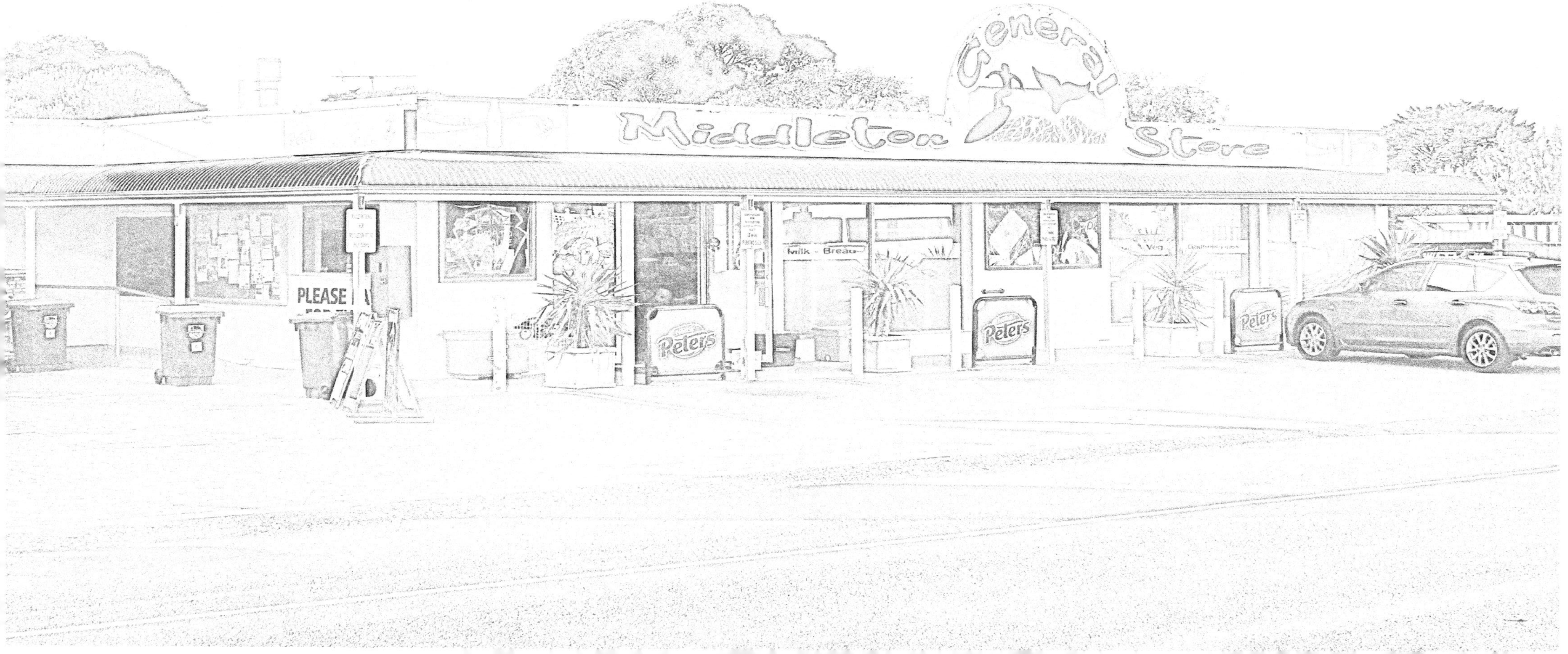
General
Middleton
Store
Milk - Bread
Peters
Peters
Peters
Peters
PLEASE

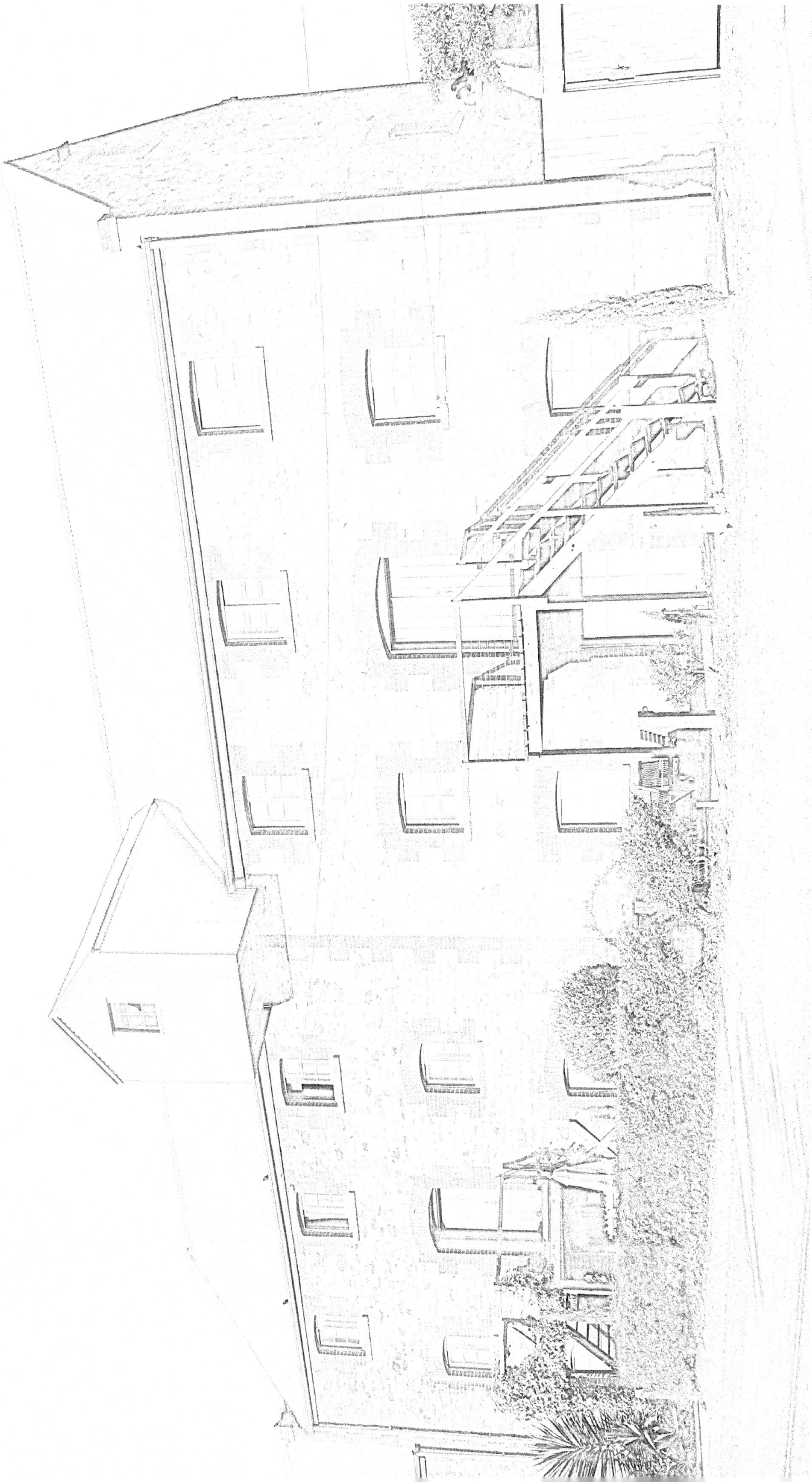

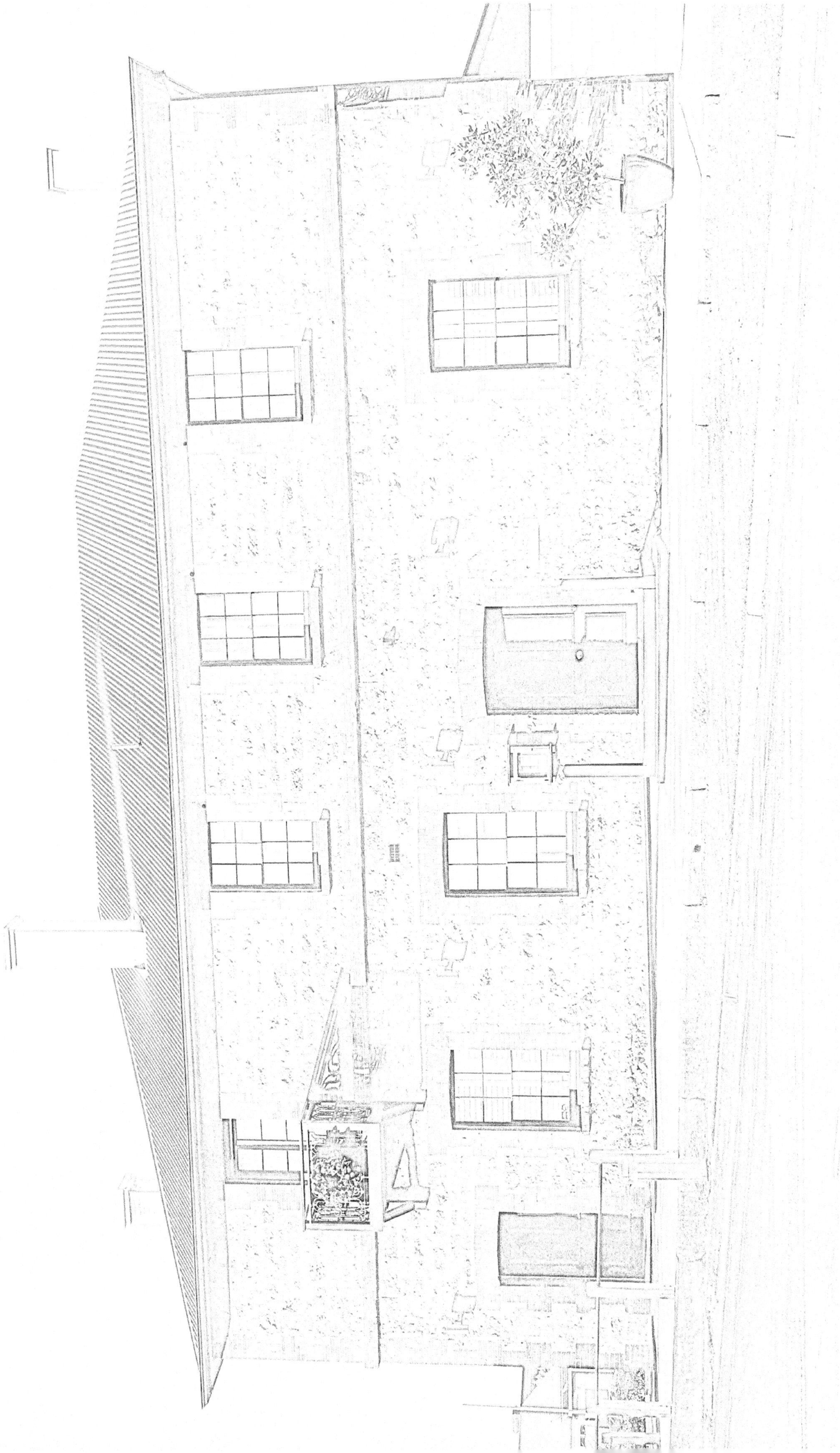

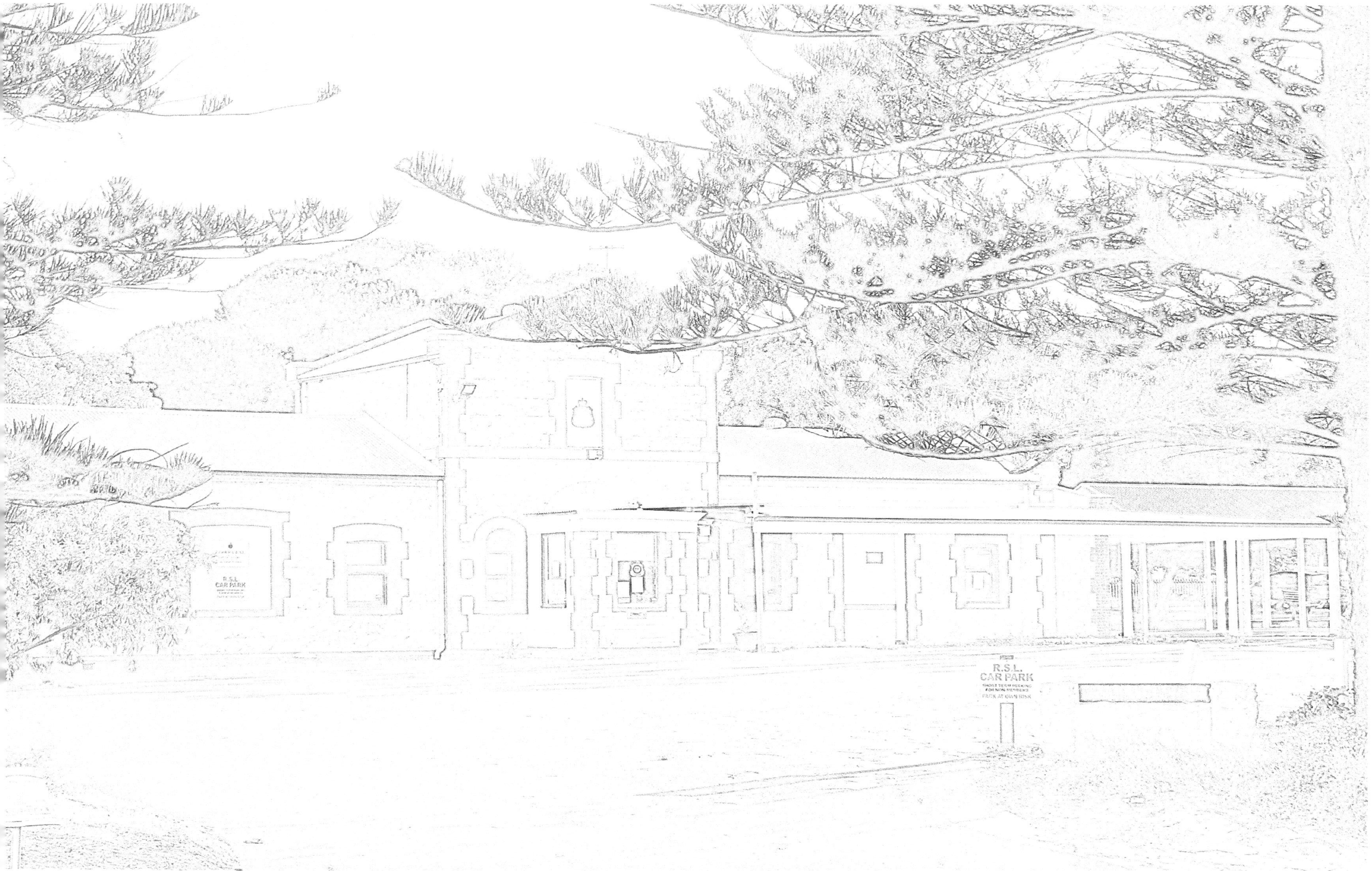
R.S.L.
CAR PARK
SHORT TERM PARKING
FOR NON MEMBERS
PARK AT OWN RISK
R.S.L.
CAR PARK

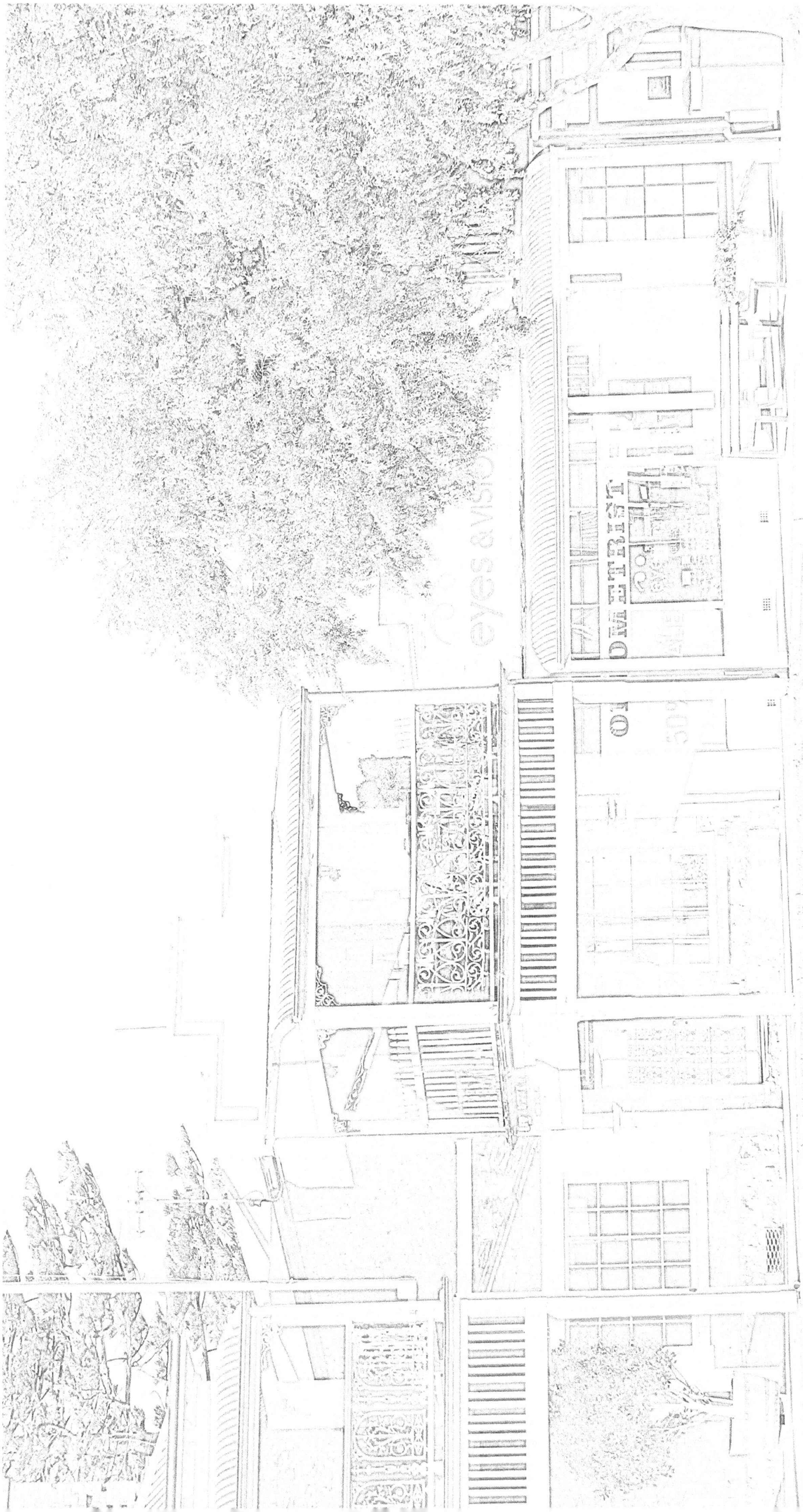

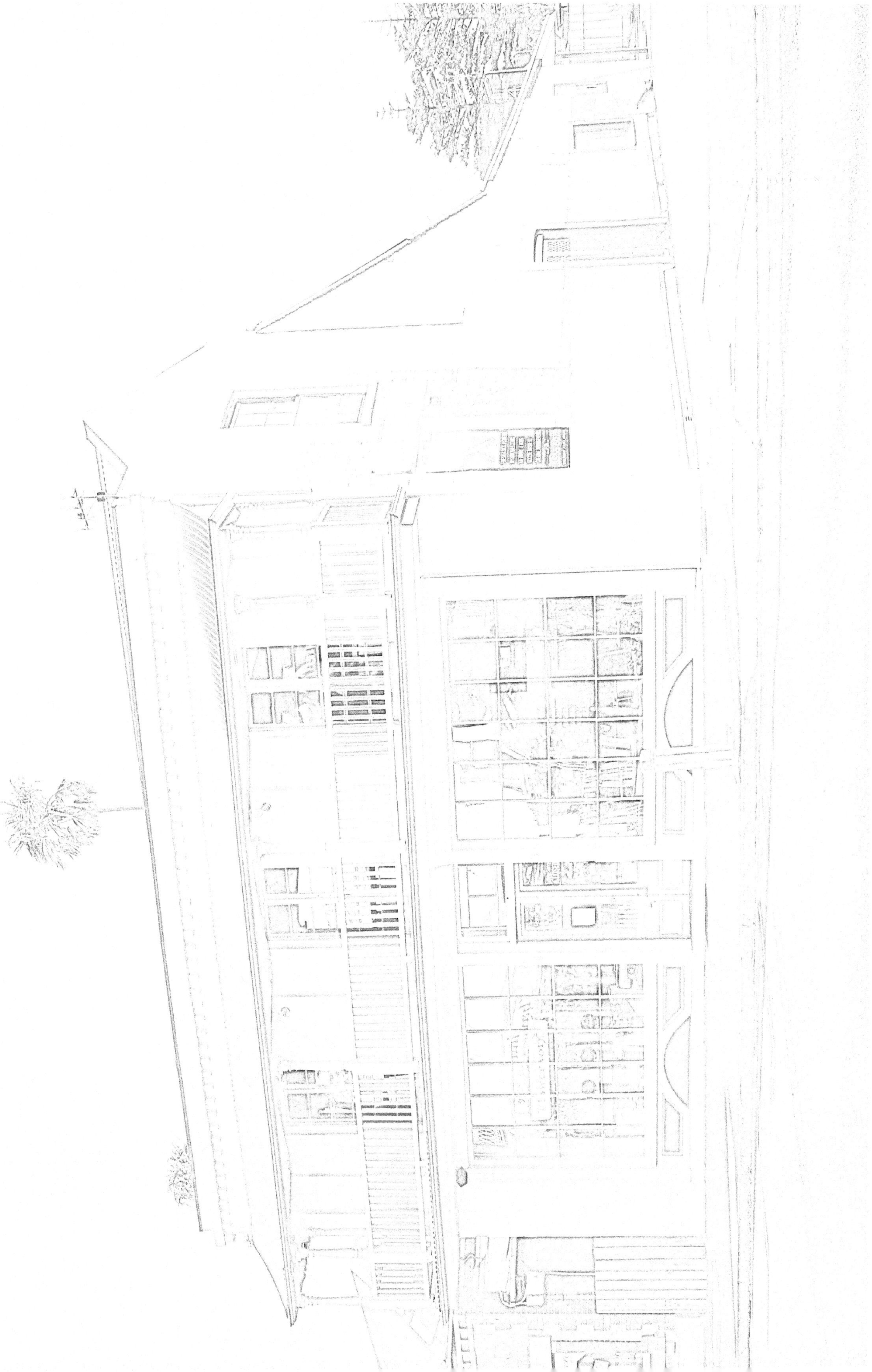

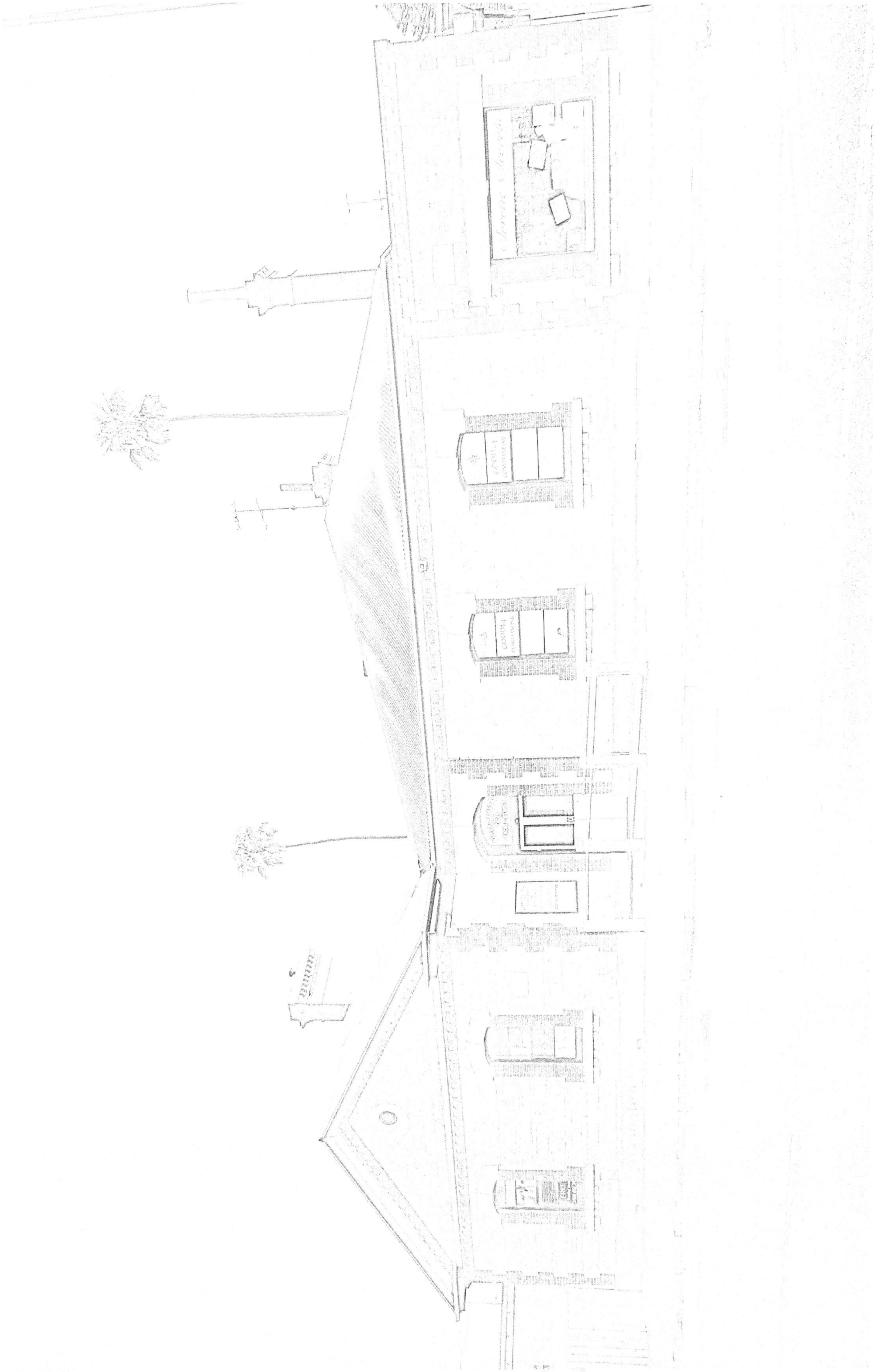

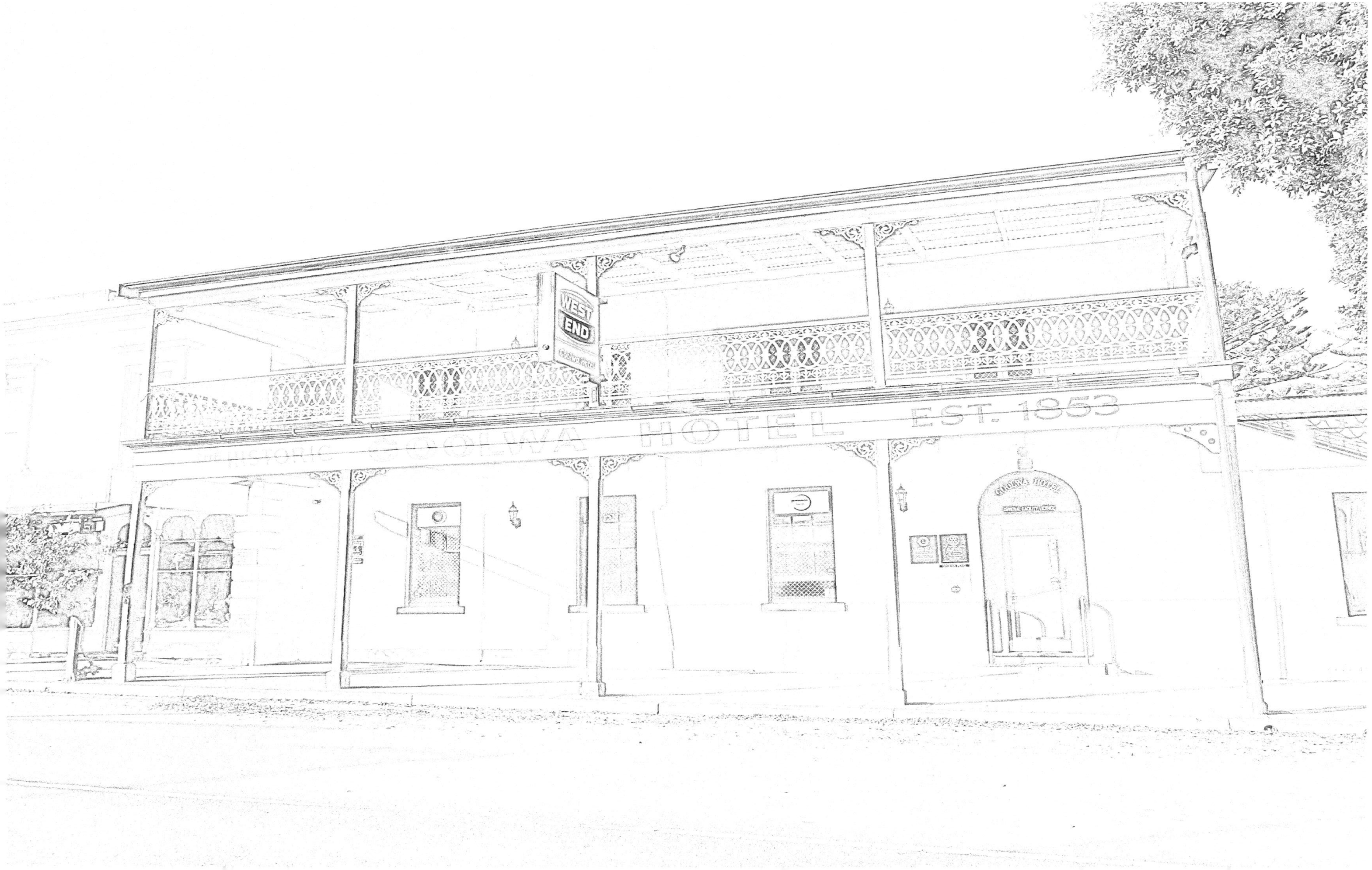
WEST END
HOTEL EST. 1853

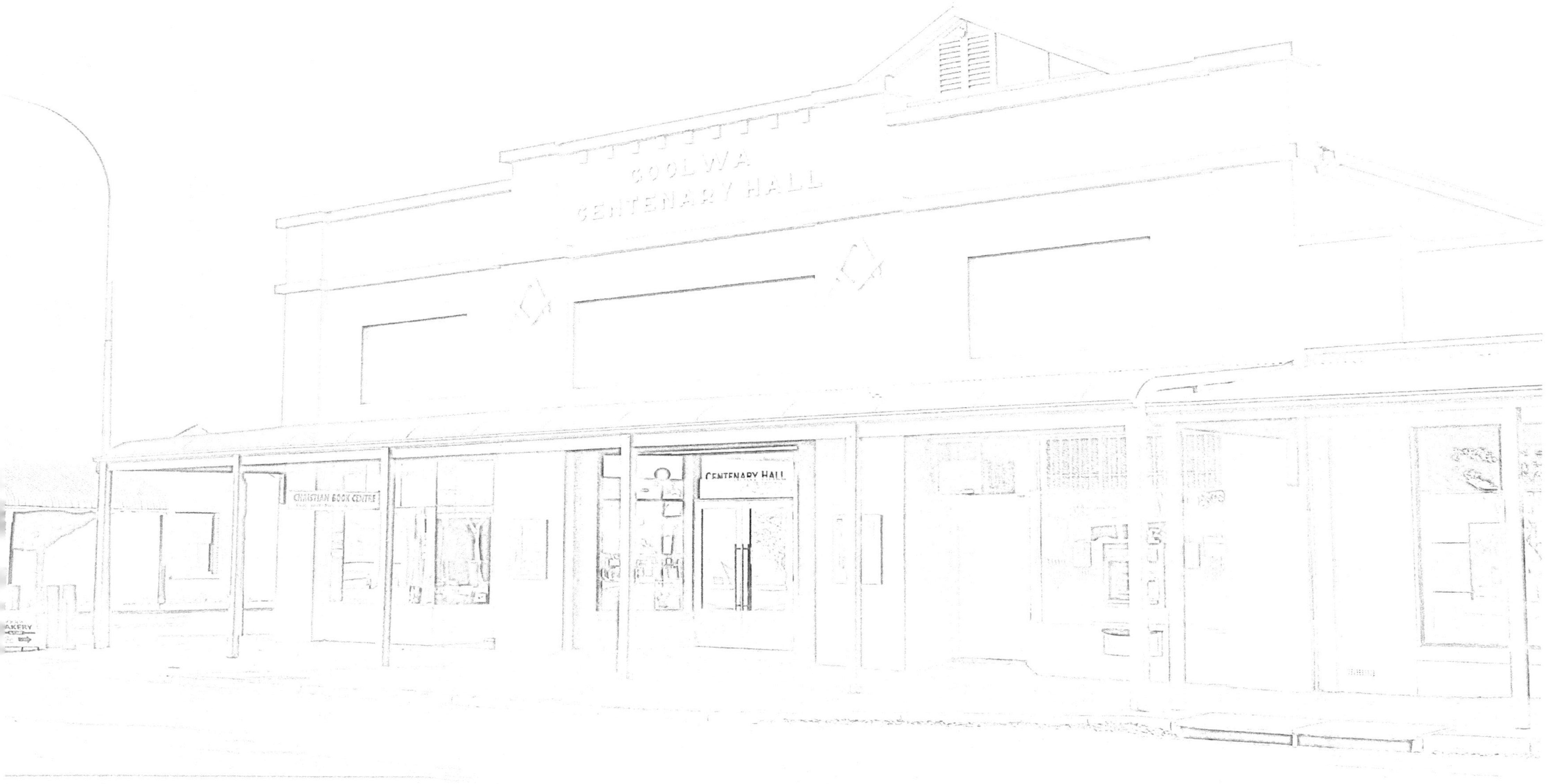
GOOLWA
CENTENARY HALL
CENTENARY HALL
CHRISTIAN BOOK CENTRE
AKERY

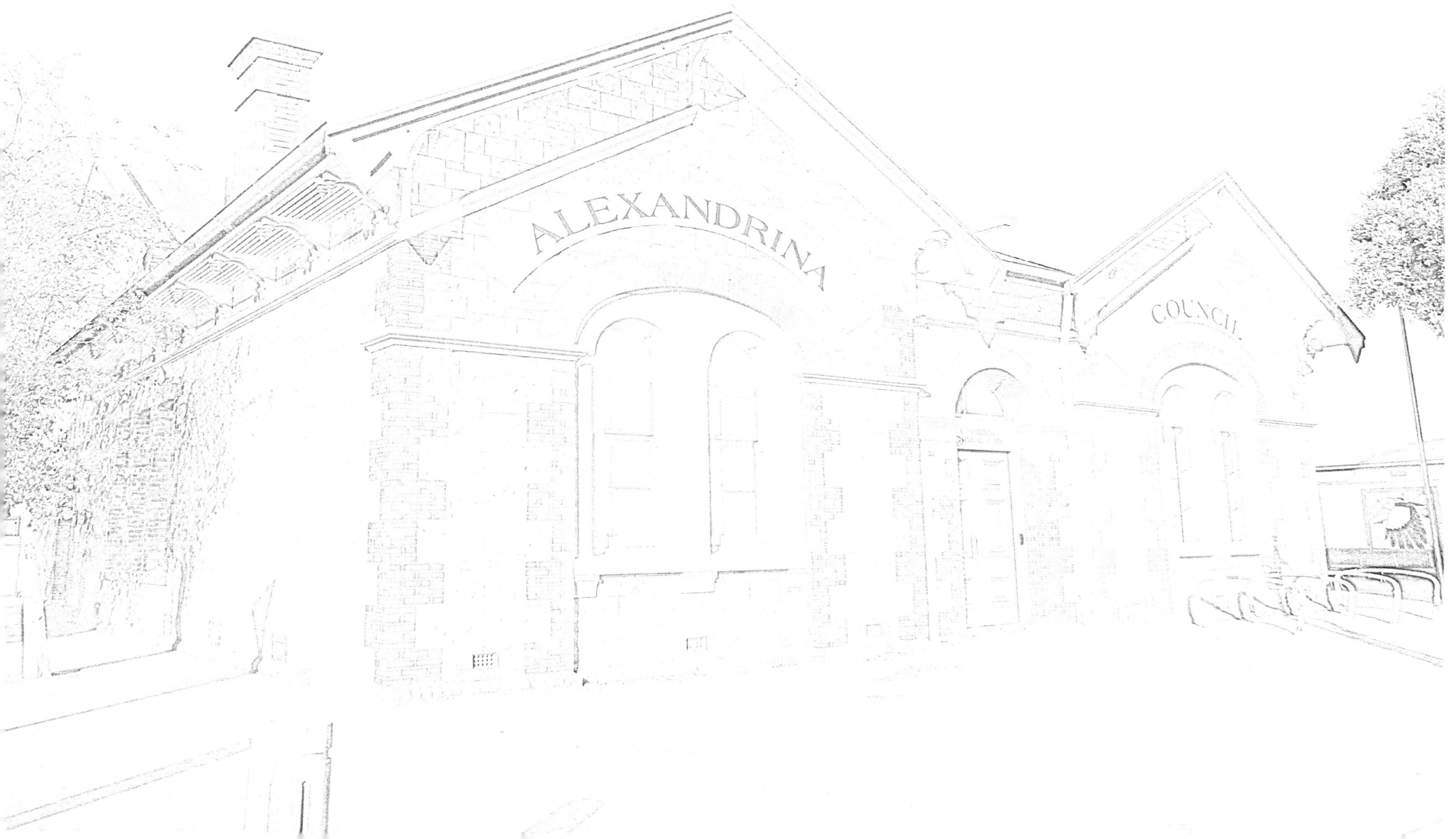
ALEXANDRINA
COUNCIL

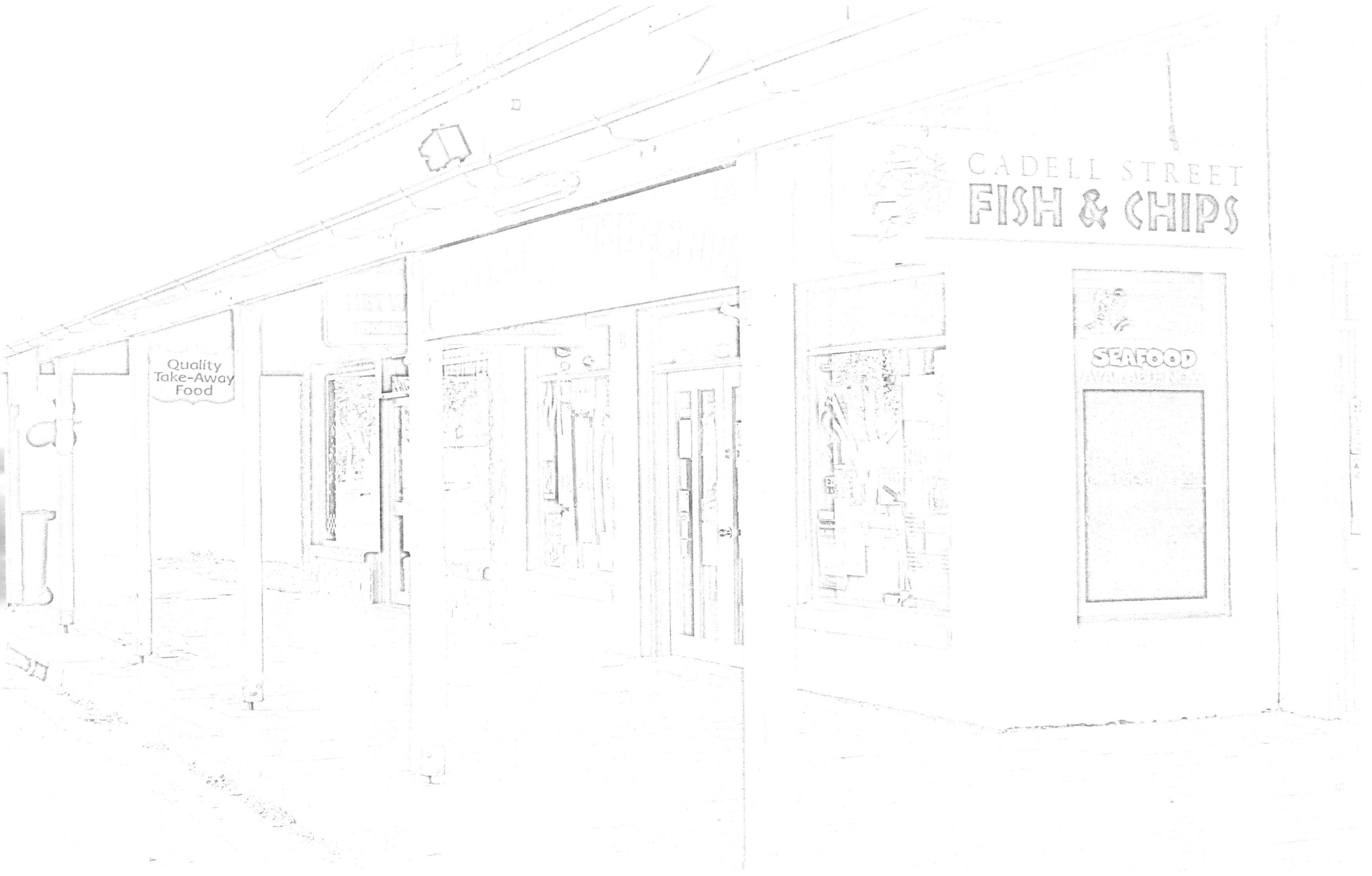
CADELL STREET
FISH & CHIPS
SEAFOOD
Quality
Take-Away
Food

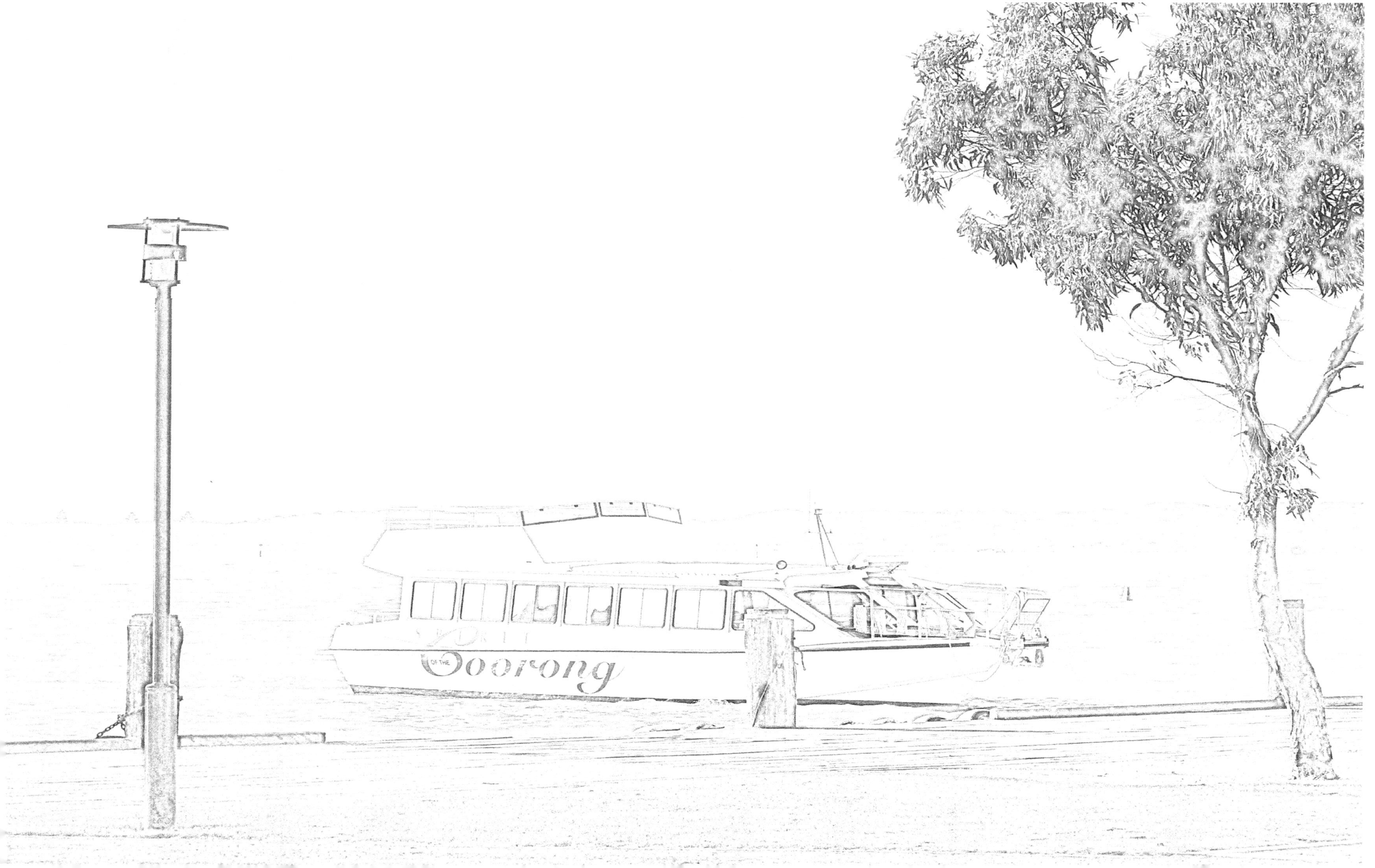
OF THE Coorong

www.ingramcontent.com/pod-product-compliance
Lightning Source LLC
Chambersburg PA
CBHW081058180526
45170CB00005B/1799